TALKING WITH CONFIDENCE

DON GABOR is an author, communications trainer, and 'small talk' expert. He has been writing and speaking about the art of conversation since 1980 and presents workshops and keynote speeches to associations, businesses, corporations and universities. He is a member of the National Speakers Association and the American Society for Training and Development, and is a frequent media guest and spokesperson.

GW00537953

Overcoming Common Problems Series

For a full list of titles please contact
Sheldon Press, Marylebone Road, London NW1 4DU

Overcoming Common Problems Series

Overcoming Common Problems Series

Overcoming Common Problems

Talking with Confidence

Don Gabor

This edition first published in Great Britain in 1999 by
Sheldon Press, SPCK, Holy Trinity Church, Marylebone Road, London NW1 4DU

Copyright © 1997 by Don Gabor.
This edition published by arrangement with Crown Publishers, Inc., New York.

British Library Cataloguing-in-Publication Data
A catalogue record for this book is available from the British Library

ISBN 0–85969–813–0

Typeset by Deltatype Ltd, Birkenhead, Merseyside
Printed in Great Britain by
Biddles Ltd, Guildford and King's Lynn

Contents

Dedication and Acknowledgements

My special thanks go to my wife, Eileen Cowell, for her superb editing and support throughout this project. I also want to thank my family, my friends, and office cat Sophie for their continued enthusiasm and inspiration.

Finally, I dedicate this book to every shy person motivated to improve his or her ability to communicate.

Introduction

Shyness – the bane of your existence – rears its ugly head yet once again! Perhaps it is when a friend at work says, 'We're having a party next weekend. Would you like to come?' Or maybe your stomach knots up when your boss chooses you to make a stand-up presentation at a meeting. Or a sudden case of 'dry mouth' twists your tongue into a reef knot during a job interview.

If you consider yourself shy, you are not alone. Studies show that more than 75 per cent of adults consider themselves 'shy' in one or more social and business situations. In fact, many people are not just shy about public speaking, but are terrified to enter a roomful of strangers, meet new people, and start conversations.

How this book can help you

Talking with Confidence is a book about 'speaking in public'. It presents proven techniques that I have taught to thousands of shy people – professionals, students, singles and couples – who have attended my conversation workshops since 1980. I know these communication skills work because I personally use them in every social and business conversation I encounter. Based on the hundreds of letters I have received from past students and readers, I know these 'tried and tested' skills can help even the most reluctant communicator to become more open and talkative.

As you master the skills in this book, you will conquer the butterflies you feel in your stomach every time you meet and talk to others in social and business situations. This hands-on guide provides the communication tools for getting past your shyness and building the confidence you need to talk with poise and power. Each chapter shows you how to overcome nervousness, fear of rejection, and even potential hostility, when talking in small and large groups. Easy-to-follow examples and exercises demonstrate dozens of surefire communication skills, tips and techniques. The primary objective of this book is to help you conquer shyness and talk confidently in every social and business situation.

How to use this book

Talking with Confidence is divided into three parts: Part 1: 'Kicking the shyness habit', Part 2: 'Speaking in social situations', and Part 3: 'Speaking in business situations'. You can start at the beginning and read all the way through to the end or instead choose a specific chapter that addresses your particular need. Part 1 focuses on getting over what has probably been a lifelong problem – chronic shyness. In three short chapters you'll learn how to break the shyness habit by changing the way you talk to yourself, sharing your expertise and interests, and showing your sense of humour.

Part 2 focuses on informal social situations in which you can interact and express yourself more effectively. In six concise chapters you'll learn how to master small talk, mingle at parties, hold a get-together, extricate yourself from uncomfortable conversations, propose toasts, and even build relationships on the telephone.

Part 3 concentrates on communicating with clarity and assurance in more formal business environments. In these nine jam-packed chapters you'll learn how to present well at an interview for a new job, conduct a meeting, present a speech, 'soft-sell', negotiate, deal with difficult clients, facilitate a training session, talk business over meals, and network at conventions.

Getting started

Some shy people have told me that they feel less inhibited in business situations than in social situations because in business everyone knows what to expect from one another. It's the small talk and mingling at parties that drives shy people to distraction. But others say that social situations are easier to cope with because of more relaxed rules of etiquette. Whether you are nervous and inhibited in social or business situations, remember that you can learn to relax and be more outgoing. If you are ready to change your life, then just turn the page and start learning how to break the shyness habit. It will surprise you how easily you can master these skills and get what you want out of life simply by *Talking with Confidence!*

Part 1 Kicking the shyness habit

1

Changing the way you talk to yourself

Stop reinforcing your shy behaviour

Everyone has embarrassing moments at one time or another. Think of how you feel when you meet a new person in a social or business situation. Do you get uncomfortable, tongue-tied and nervous? Do your palms sweat and do you blush, giggle or say ridiculous things? Is it pure agony to make small talk and carry on a conversation? Are you afraid of sounding foolish or offending the other person? Do you want to escape from the situation as quickly as possible? If responses such as these occur on a regular basis when you meet people, then you probably describe yourself as 'shy'.

Although you have been reserved for most of your life, there is a way to kick the shyness habit. You may not realize it, but how you talk to yourself plays a significant role in your level of shyness. When that little voice inside your head starts planting those old seeds of doubt, your nervous reactions are not far behind. This deflating 'self-talk' depletes your confidence and reinforces shy behaviour.

Replace inhibiting 'self-talk' with confidence-building statements

The first step in breaking your pattern of shy behaviour is to change how you talk to yourself. By replacing shy and often detrimental self-talk with confidence-building statements, you can initiate the process of changing how you feel. Whenever you hear that destructive voice in your head start to undermine your confidence, say to yourself, 'Stop!' Then decide to replace subverting self-talk with constructive statements that build your self-esteem. The following chart shows typical shy self-talk and the words you can say instead to increase your confidence.

STOP saying to yourself:	*START saying to yourself:*
'I never know what to say.'	*'I'll show interest in others.'*
'I hate meeting new people.'	*'I want to make some new friends.'*
'I can't do it.'	*'I'll try it and see what happens.'*

'I don't want to go to the party.'	*'I might meet someone interesting.'*
'I probably won't have any fun.'	*'I can be amusing when I want to be.'*
'I'm boring.'	*'I'll discuss some of my interests.'*
'No one will want to talk to me.'	*'I'll be the first to say hello.'*
'I wish I were better looking.'	*'I may not be perfect, but who is?'*
'This is an absolute waste of time.'	*'What do I have to lose?'*
'I always say the most ridiculous things.'	*'It's how I say it that counts.'*

Three steps to rehearse constructive self-talk

You can do three things to make constructive self-talk easier.

Step 1: Find a quiet time and location where others won't interrupt you

First, establish a daily routine in which you can practise how you talk to yourself. Find a few quiet times and places during the day where you can spend a few tranquil minutes alone. Good times to rehearse are before breakfast, while you exercise, during breaks, after work, on walks, while you relax in the evening, or just before you go to sleep. The more you practise constructive self-talk, the faster you can change your shy behaviour.

Step 2: Visualize a specific situation

Second, consider a situation that's coming up in which you will probably feel inhibited. For example, perhaps you always get tongue-tied at your department's weekly meeting. Now use your imagination to visualize the situation as clearly as possible. See your colleagues making small talk while they wait for your supervisor to start the meeting. Notice where people sit and imagine what they are saying to each other. See how the meeting progresses and imagine what everyone says and does. The secret to effective visualizations is to fill in as many minute details as possible, including the time, room temperature, what people are wearing, and even their facial expressions.

Step 3: Picture and describe your constructive actions, attitudes and feelings in the situation

Imagine yourself interacting in a more outgoing manner with your fellow workers and supervisor under these circumstances. Meticulously describe your actions, attitudes and feelings in constructive terms and in the present tense. If a negative thought creeps in, acknowledge it as a confidence-buster and swiftly substitute it with positive self-talk. While visualizing a staff meeting, you might say to yourself:

'I want to ask an important question during the meeting.'

'I can help other people in my department to be more efficient.'

'These weekly meetings are much more interesting when I share my ideas.'

'My confidence shows when I actively participate and help solve problems.'

'I feel like part of our team when I co-operate and contribute during the meeting.'

Changing the way you talk to yourself creates a more positive self-image

In the past, your shy self-talk resulted in shy behaviour, but now you are starting to learn how to use constructive self-talk to create a more confident and outgoing manner. To overcome your shyness, you can write a new self-talk script and then practise it before each situation in which you expect to feel uncomfortable. By describing the positive actions, attitudes and feelings you want to experience *before* they occur, you will gain confidence and poise.

You may be surprised at how quickly you can shatter that old pattern of shyness and become a more outspoken individual. You'll know that your constructive self-talk is working when in social and business situations you sit tall, walk tall, and seem self-assured. You will feel your confidence grow as your conversation becomes more creative and spontaneous. It all starts with the way you talk to yourself. Constructive self-talk changes the way you feel about yourself and sets the stage for kicking the shyness habit.

FIFTEEN WAYS TO OVERCOME SHYNESS

1 Stop depending on others to communicate for you in social or business situations.
2 Expand your social life outside the family.
3 Visualize yourself as an active, interested and interesting conversationalist.
4 Find and emulate good conversationalists.
5 Use relaxation techniques before you go into social and business situations.
6 Gain conversational momentum by always practising your communication skills.
7 Identify your conversational successes and pat yourself on the back.
8 Create a socializing schedule for yourself and stick to it.
9 Avoid judging yourself too harshly if you make a mistake or say the wrong thing.
10 Identify how others respond to you and keep doing what gets positive results.
11 Validate others by acknowledging their achievements and self-worth.
12 Graciously accept compliments by saying, 'Thanks for saying so. I appreciate hearing that.'
13 Talk to people who make you feel good about yourself.
14 Focus more on the other person than on yourself.
15 Give others the benefit of the doubt and they will do the same for you.

2

Turning your shyness into an asset

Share your strengths, interests and passions

List your strengths instead of your weaknesses and use them to become a more confident communicator. As a shy person, you may spend more time alone than you would like, but it does give you opportunities to develop several interests and abilities. In the past you may have pursued these endeavours alone, but now you can break that pattern and share them with others.

The best way to begin is to ask yourself specific questions. What do you do well? What are you passionate about? So you have 'green fingers'? Can you identify a valuable antique or collectable at a car boot sale or garage sale? Is music, art or sports your passion? As you list your interests, always remember that what you do in life and your level of expertise in a chosen field is not as important as your willingness to share your enthusiasm and knowledge with the people you meet. On a sheet of paper, list some of your skills, passions, hobbies and interests. Then write various ways you might use your abilities to help someone or to expand your contacts with others.

Now choose just *one* way you can share your skills or expertise with a person or a group. For example, showing a new employee the 'ropes' or joining a skittles or darts league is an easy, low-risk way to chip away at your shyness. As you feel more confident, offer to conduct a team activity at work or volunteer to teach a course or workshop in your area of expertise at a local recreation centre. When you demonstrate that you are willing to share your interests and strengths with others, people will admire and appreciate you. Your self-esteem will soar along with your confidence, and you'll naturally feel less shy and more talkative because you're involved in something that you feel enthusiastic about.

'Blow your own trumpet' without sounding egotistical

You may feel reluctant to tell others about your abilities out of fear of sounding like a show-off. Perhaps you are loth to reveal your

7

I LIKE AND AM GOOD AT:

- Using a computer art program.
- Planning and completing long-term projects at work.
- Plumbing, electrical and other home repairs.
- Playing football and table tennis.
- Playing the guitar.
- Identifying valuable coins and stamps.
- Cooking an inexpensive gourmet meal.

I CAN SHARE THESE INTERESTS AND STRENGTHS WITH OTHERS BY:

- Helping a new person at work learn a computer program.
- Discussing with a colleague the possibility of working together on future projects.
- Teaching an adult-education course on easy home repairs.
- Organizing a local football game or table tennis tournament.
- Offering to teach a new friend a few guitar lessons.
- Inviting an interested acquaintance to attend a coin and stamp fair.
- Asking a new friend to go to cookery classes.

accomplishments because you think that others might perceive you as conceited. Actually, if you 'blow your own trumpet' gently, the opposite usually happens. Most people want to know something interesting and unique about you. This helps them understand what you are willing to talk about and if you have anything in common with them. Remember, many people are just as shy as you, so letting them in on your passions or obsessions helps them to feel more comfortable when talking to you. For example, at a party when someone asks me what I like to do, I reply with something like:

'I'm a book person. I write books. I love to read books. I sell books. Books are my life!'

This answer usually evokes a question or two about the kinds of books I write and enjoy reading. After a few more thoughts about books and publishing, I make sure that the other person is also interested in this topic by inquiring, 'What kind of books do you enjoy reading?' or 'Are you interested in writing and publishing too?'

To let others know that you are willing to share your expertise, follow these examples:

'Oh, you want to learn how to play backgammon? I play with friends every weekend. If you want, I can show you the basic moves and strategies.'

'If you'd like a few guitar lessons, just let me know. I used to play in a band.'

'I heard you mention that you want to buy a used car, but you're afraid it might be a dud. I'm pretty good when it comes to fixing cars. I'd be happy to look at the car for you and tell you what I think of its condition.'

A few words of caution about sharing your expertise

Avoid talking too much about a particularly esoteric subject, offering too much unsolicited advice, discussing obscure concepts, using complicated terms and jargon, or exaggerating your abilities or achievements.

Playing the expert helps you kick the shyness habit

When you talk about your passions and pursuits, your shyness takes a backseat. Those old butterflies may still crop up on occasion, but letting others in on your interests can do wonders to boost your confidence. New friends and old acquaintances will see you as a friendly person who enjoys sharing your expertise and enthusiasm with others.

Express Your Views Without Sounding Opinionated

Do you sometimes get into disagreements while sharing your views? Or do you conceal your beliefs because you do not want to sound opinionated? Use the chart below to adjust your conversational style when expressing your opinions.

Encourages Constructive Exchange	Sounds Closed and Opinionated
• Discuss many sides of an issue before forming a conclusion.	• Present a narrow viewpoint without seeing other possibilities.
• Acknowledge another viewpoint even if it is different from yours.	• Deny the validity of other viewpoints and feelings.
• Accept that others may disagree.	• Interrupt and do not listen.
• Encourage others to express their opposing views.	• Make personal attacks.
• Support your views with facts.	• Make emotional generalizations.
• Find areas of agreement with others.	• Argue over minor details and turn the conversation into a debate.

3

Using humour to overcome shyness

Humour is where you find it

For a shy person, there's nothing funny about being uncomfortable in social situations, but using your sense of humour can help you become more outgoing and gregarious. Making a pun or a quip, or telling a short lighthearted story, adds zest to your conversations and encourages others to chime in with a joke of their own. Researchers have shown that humour really does work to decrease anxiety in social and business situations alike because laughter makes people more relaxed and receptive.

If you are like many shy people, you've got a good sense of humour, but you may be reluctant to show it. However, sharing a laugh with someone you've just met will make both of you feel more comfortable in the first few minutes of conversation. This easy-going attitude decreases your shyness and makes you appear more appealing and attractive.

Listen for the humour around you

You don't have to be the first one to crack a joke to show your sense of humour. There are many easy ways to share what tickles your funny bone. One way is to react to a clever or amusing remark. You need to be honest with your reactions, though, so don't fake a laugh if you don't think what you heard is funny. However, a sincere smile and laugh at a quip or amusing story sends a powerful signal of approval and makes the speaker feel good about talking to you. Listen carefully for droll remarks, dry wit, whimsical stories, puns, plays on words, or anything else that you can respond to with a chuckle or chortle. Your smile and laugh at someone's jest compliments him or her and shows you are listening.

You can also reveal that you appreciate someone else's sense of humour by stating the obvious – 'You're funny!' or 'You've got a great sense of humour'. This friendly comment encourages that person to open up to you. When you respond to humour in a conversation, you send this message to the speaker:

'I like you and I enjoy your perspective. Thanks for sharing it with me.'

Reveal your sense of humour by telling an amusing story

Can you remember some of the most amusing moments you've observed at a party, a wedding, or in another situation where something happened that made everyone laugh? For example, during our wedding reception in our back garden, my best man tossed a piece of melba toast into the air as he wished my bride and me a happy life together. Unexpectedly, the airborne 'toast' sailed into the fish pond. The guests howled!

Perhaps you have witnessed a bloomer during an important event that left people laughing hysterically. To add humour to a conversation, tell funny real-life situations like these. Everyone has amusing stories to tell. The point is, you can share your sense of humour without being a stand-up comedian or clown. A few mildly amusing anecdotes or *short* stories, which are real and easily related, can get people laughing. The closer the story relates to the topic of conversation, the funnier it will be.

For a list of possible amusing situations, see the bulleted list at the end of this chapter.

Use self-effacing humour

Another way you can show your sense of humour is to recount a funny episode that happened to *you*. Telling a story about how you handled an embarrassing or an awkward situation is a powerful communication tool, both in social and business situations. When you laugh at yourself, you convey confidence and poise. Maybe this is why so many successful speakers, entertainers and business leaders use this form of humour to build rapport with their audiences. A modest amount of self-effacing humour shows you are not oversensitive about your weaknesses or past mistakes. When you can poke fun at yourself, you are telling everyone that you feel comfortable and confident.

The following are good examples of how some famous people poke fun at themselves.

Ava Gardner is rumoured to have said this about herself:

'Deep down I'm pretty superficial.'

A telegram from Groucho Marx to the exclusive Friars Club in Hollywood:

'Please accept my resignation. I don't want to belong to any club that would accept me as a member.'

The three biggest mistakes to avoid when using humour

1 Sexual and ethnic jokes, and jokes about the disabled, are inappropriate and can offend.
2 Sarcastic humour, if unchecked, alienates and offends because people take it personally.
3 Practical jokes can lead to accidents and be the kiss of death for a budding career.

Kicking the shyness habit pays off fast

You might think that 'old habits die hard', but with practice you can quickly change how you react and feel in social and business situations. Writing your own script of constructive 'self-talk', sharing your expertise with others, and using your sense of humour can do wonders to boost your confidence. While in the past you often felt uncomfortable meeting new people, now you will know how to overcome shyness and make every conversation an enjoyable and rewarding experience.

AMUSING SITUATIONS THAT LEAD TO LAUGHS

Everyone has embarrassing or amusing moments that they can share with others. To help you remember a few funny stories, consider this list of common situations that may lend themselves to humorous retelling.

- A case of mistaken identity.
- A mistaken telephone call.
- A mix-up in gifts.
- A family get-together.
- An event at work or at school.
- An event on the beach or in a swimming pool.
- An important meeting.
- An unusual birthday party celebration.
- What happened with an article of clothing.
- A first day in a job.
- An event in a fitness class.
- A faux pas at a hotel or restaurant.
- A blind date.
- A most embarrassing moment.
- An event described in the news.
- Something your child or pet did.
- A time when you were trying to be sophisticated.
- An event that is funny now, but wasn't when it happened.

Part 2 Speaking in social situations

4

Mastering the art of small talk

Small talk creates a friendly atmosphere

Small talk is light and casual conversation that avoids obscure subjects, arguments or emotionally charged issues. If you are like many shy people, you might think small talk is a waste of time, but nothing could be further from the truth! Making small talk is an easy way to get to know someone, create a positive first impression, and gain self-confidence.

Discussing general-interest subjects such as films, music, theatre, sport, books, food, travel, etc. demonstrates to others that you are approachable and friendly. When you offer a few lighthearted comments or ask and answer questions, you send the message that you are ready, willing and able to communicate. This is especially critical for other shy people who look for a 'green light' or extra encouragement before they even consider participating in a conversation. When you make casual conversation, other shy people will conclude that you are a person with whom they can easily converse.

Small talk allows for an informal exchange of basic information

One highly useful aspect of small talk is that it enables two people to learn a great deal about each other in a short amount of time. Small talk provides an opportunity for you to casually find out where people are from, what they do for pleasure and profit – even what they love to eat or what their lifelong dreams are. In addition, if you listen carefully, you will discover that most people readily reveal the topics they want to discuss or subjects in which they are interested.

When you hear an interesting remark, acknowledge it with a comment and an easy-to-answer follow-up question. For example, if an acquaintance mentions a recent holiday, you might respond, 'I know exactly what you mean about travelling because it's one of my hobbies too! What made you decide to visit . . . ?' Small talk is a confidence-booster because it enables you and your conversational

17

partner to quickly find areas of common interest and helps you choose topics that both of you feel comfortable discussing.

Ten steps to mastering small talk

Have you ever wondered how some people can enter a roomful of strangers and strike up a conversation with practically anyone? Even if you are shy, the secret to pulling off this communication coup is easy if you follow these ten steps.

Step 1: Before the event, identify several interests and experiences that you are willing to discuss

Can you imagine a marathon runner not warming up before a big race or a barrister improvising to the jury the key points of an important case? In each situation, preparation is the key to success. The same is true for mastering small talk. For the shy person, the first critical step in mastering small talk is preparing what *you* want to talk about. By identifying at least six or more 'hot' topics and stimulating experiences, you can prime your 'conversational pump' and get ready to communicate. To list possible topics, ask yourself questions such as:

'What have I read lately that I enjoyed or found thought-provoking?'

'What film, play or performance amused me or captured my imagination?'

'What restaurants could I recommend to someone who shares my tastes in food?'

'What recordings or concerts have I heard that may interest other music lovers?'

'What are my current hobbies?'

'What plans do I have for this weekend or for my next holiday?'

'What insights can I share about my business or work that might be interesting?'

18

You may be reluctant to talk to strangers or previous acquaintances, but once you make this exercise part of your mental preparation for socializing, you will never be at a loss for words when the opportunity to converse arises. In addition, you'll discover many other people who share your interests and are willing to talk about what they enjoy.

Hint: When you first meet a person, avoid the following unpleasant, overly personal or highly controversial issues because they can quickly degenerate into depressing conversations or arguments:

- Personal, health, money or family problems.
- Divorce or death.
- Gory crimes and the decaying moral values of Western civilization.
- Lay-offs, redundancies and gloomy economic predictions.
- Terrorism, war, diseases and famine.
- Emotionally charged issues such as abortion, social security benefits or capital punishment.
- Sex, politics and religion.

Step 2: Search for individuals who seem receptive

From the moment you enter a room, search for people who are already talking or appear as though they want to talk. These people are usually the easiest ones to approach because they require little prodding to engage in conversation.

Step 3: Establish eye contact and smile to send receptive signals

Casual eye contact and a warm, friendly smile demonstrate your interest and desire to communicate. Eye contact for five to ten seconds indicates curiosity and is generally considered friendly. Take care not to stare at another person too intensely because this can make him or her feel uncomfortable. When the other person returns the eye contact, smile back. At that point you have made a connection and transmitted the message that you want to have a conversation.

This first contact is usually the precise moment when most shy people become nervous, fold their arms, and avert their gaze. Avoid 'mixed signals' in which you make eye contact and then look away for several minutes. The other person often interprets this as a loss of interest. He or she may think that you looked, and then did not like what you saw.

Hint: To neutralize your nervousness and communicate receptivity, unfold your arms, move your hands completely away from your face (including your mouth and chin), and smile. By keeping your body language open and relaxed, you'll send out confident and friendly signals that say you are available for contact.

Step 4: Be the first to introduce yourself and ask an easy, open-ended question

Do you hang back and wait for others to start a conversation with you? The problem with this passive strategy is that the longer you wait, the more nervous and uncomfortable you will become. Instead, move into an action mode. Take the initiative and be the first to say hello. This not only demonstrates confidence and shows interest in the other person, but it gives you the opportunity to guide the conversation. Most people in social situations are perfectly delighted to chat if someone approaches them in an easy-going way. Begin your conversation by introducing yourself. Then follow with an easy-to-answer question about something in your immediate surroundings. In most cases, 'open-ended' questions are best because they elicit detailed responses. The following are examples of open-ended questions that will encourage the other person to talk:

'How do you know our host?'

'What do you think of this spectacular view?'

'Could you explain to me how this . . . works?'

You can also launch a conversation by offering a sincere compliment with a follow-up question, or by making a lighthearted comment. As a rule, the earlier you introduce yourself in a conversation, the better. When you come to a pause in your conversation, smile, make eye contact, shake hands, and say, 'By the way, my name is . . .'

Hint: Be aware of cultural differences in what is considered a comfortable communicating distance. For most people and cultures, a span of about three feet between new acquaintances is about right.

20

Step 5: Listen carefully for the other person's name, and then use it in the conversation

Even the most gregarious people often forget the names of the people they meet. The reason is that they are either thinking of what they are going to say next or are focused on making a good impression. For a shy person like you, mastering the ability to remember names quickly boosts your conversational power and really impresses the people you meet.

While I'm no memory expert, my ability to remember first names is good. Here is what I do to remember the first name of someone I've just met:

- At the moment of introduction I focus only on his or her name and face.
- I immediately repeat the person's name to make sure that I got it right.
- If I missed the name, I ask the person to repeat it.
- I quickly think of someone I know with the same name.
- I say the name periodically in the conversation.
- I always use the person's name when I close the conversation.

Step 6: Listen carefully for facts, feelings, key words, free information and implied statements

Another powerful tool to help you make small talk with strangers is active listening. Tune into facts, feelings, key words, free information and implied statements that suggest topics of interest or common experiences. Listen for phrases or words that create a mental picture. For example, '... going on a dream holiday', '... excited about a new job', '... rescued an abandoned dog', 'I can't wait to ...' When you hear a word or phrase that triggers a picture, simply ask something like, 'You mentioned that you spent time in York. What were you doing there?' or say, 'York! That's where I grew up. Did you enjoy working there?'

Listening between the lines tells you what not to say

When listening 'between the lines' you may hear implied statements that suggest emotionally charged topics to avoid. Since many people often reveal their feelings unconsciously and indirectly, listening is

21

your primary tool for knowing what and what not to say. If a person implies or states a negative feeling about a particular topic, avoiding that topic is probably wise. For example, if I heard someone I had just met in a social situation say any of the following comments, I would quickly change the subject to something more positive:

> *'After the idiots I worked for sacked everyone in our depart-ment . . .'*

> *'I couldn't wait to get out of that terrible marriage, so I . . .'*

> *'Do you want to know what I really hate?'*

> *'Don't get me going on that!'*

Step 7: Disclose some of your background, interests and experiences

If you only ask questions and never share anything about yourself, your contact with others will be more like interrogations than conversations. Therefore, it is essential to tell people about yourself. However, don't overwhelm them with your life story or list your accomplishments as if you were being interviewed for a job. Casually pepper your conversation with a bit of your background and experience, and you will reveal who you are in a positive and interesting way. For example:

> *'When I was growing up in . . .'*

> *'In my spare time I enjoy . . .'*

> *'I've been working as a . . . for many years.'*

Hint: Let the other person know of any interests or experiences that you think you may have in common.

Step 8: Explore the other person's interests by encouraging him or her to talk

Revealing information about your hobbies, job or family makes it easy for others to know what you want to talk about. However, you do not want to prattle endlessly about yourself. Keep small talk stimulating by changing topics at the right time. This is effortless if you have made a point to listen for facts, key words, free information, feelings and implied statements. Simply say, 'I heard you mention earlier . . .' or 'It's funny that you brought up that subject. I'm interested in that, too.' Or you can merely change the subject by inquiring, 'Do you mind if I ask you about something you mentioned a few minutes ago?'

Hint: While discussing a variety of issues and subjects is desirable, bouncing around too much from topic to topic is annoying. If you do leave a topic before you or the other person has finished, just pick up where the two of you left off by saying, 'Getting back to what you were saying before . . .'

Step 9: Highlight mutual interests

It may sound obvious, but one way to overcome shyness is to spend more time talking to people you like. Unfortunately, many shy people fail to cement the bonds with the likeable people they meet in social situations. That is why emphasizing areas of commonality and mutual interests is important. For example, you can say:

'It's always good to meet someone who is interested in . . .'

'I'm happy I've finally met another former pupil of . . .'

'I love it when I meet someone who is as excited about . . . as I am.'

Step 10: Restate something you found interesting in the conversation and end with an invitation to meet again

Everyone agrees that the first few minutes of contact are important, but many fail to understand that the last moments of a conversation are equally crucial. If you follow this format for ending conversations, you'll leave a positive impression on the people you meet.

First, say a few words about an interesting topic that the other person discussed. Then add that you've enjoyed the chat. Look at the person, smile, shake hands, and use his or her name. Finally, if you are so inclined, suggest that the two of you talk again soon. Offer your business card or home telephone number. Then ask the other person how you might contact him or her. The following example shows how to end a conversation the right way and leave a positive impression:

> *'Pat, it was really fun talking about the whodunnit you are reading. By the way, I belong to a crime book club where a small group of us sit around and talk about what we've been reading. If you are interested in meeting some other whodunnit buffs, I'll let you know the time and place of our next get-together. [Look for a nod, smile and agreement to this invitation.] How can I get in touch with you? Great! Well, speak to you soon then. Bye.'*

Hint: Keep your farewells short. Even if the other person does not accept your invitation, that's OK – it's still worth suggesting a future meeting, for you may not get the opportunity again.

DOS AND DON'TS FOR MAKING SMALL TALK

Do:

- ✓ Make sure people are interested in a topic before talking too much about it.
- ✓ Stick to upbeat subjects.
- ✓ Balance the amount of talking and listening.
- ✓ Find out what other people enjoy discussing.
- ✓ Be willing to talk about subjects that you know little about.
- ✓ Reintroduce yourself to an old acquaintance.

Don't:

- ✗ Indulge in endless shop talk or business gossip when non-business people are present.
- ✗ Gossip about the other guests.
- ✗ Stay in one area or speak only to one person.
- ✗ Look over a person's shoulder as you talk to him or her.
- ✗ Make negative snap judgements about the people you meet.
- ✗ Expect other people to keep the conversation going.

5

Mixing and mingling at parties

Ask who else is attending the event

Do you sometimes feel out of place at parties because you don't know anyone, or never know what to say to the other guests? Most people are uncomfortable when they enter a roomful of strangers. However, you can do several things to make socializing at parties easier and more fun.

I recently attended a semi-formal dinner at an exclusive restaurant where I knew not one person, including the host. Normally, that would be a highly nerve-racking situation, but our savvy host made our mingling much easier by sending each of us a guest list that included a few words about everyone attending the dinner party. For example, among the guests was a former politician, a psychologist, several authors and a demographics analyst. Armed with these nuggets of information, I did a little research about some of the guests. As a result, I felt much more confident and comfortable at the party, especially while we socialized before dinner.

Mixing and mingling at business and social get-togethers is easier if you know who is attending and something about them. I'm not suggesting that you spy or pry into anyone's personal affairs, but you can gather some interesting background information about their interests, hobbies, businesses or recent experiences. For example, your host might tell you that one guest recently renovated his house, that another is a budding artist about to stage her first exhibition, and that a third person helps out at a youth club.

For a shy person those first awkward moments of contact at a social event can be torture, but some prior knowledge about the other guests' interests can facilitate conversations. About a week before the event, phone the event's host or sponsor and ask him or her the following questions:

'Who are some of the other guests?' (Knowing who is attending the event can ease party jitters and help you prepare for conversations.)

'Can you tell me a little about those guests whom you think I might like to meet?' (The purpose of this question is to discover which other guests you might enjoy chatting with because you share some common interests or experiences.)

'Would you introduce me to . . . ?' (This question lets your host know that you would like a formal introduction.)

Let your host know that you appreciate his or her efforts. End your phone call with a thank-you and a comment such as 'I'm really looking forward to seeing you and meeting the other guests.'

Caution: In case it is unclear, be sure to ask your host if your invitation also includes a partner or friend.

A little research pays off

Now that you know something about the other guests, it's time to get to work. With a little reading, you can probably research enough information to carry on a conversation about a few subjects that you know are 'hot' topics for your fellow guests. Let your own curiosity and interest be your guides about how much time and effort you devote to researching a particular topic. For example, perhaps your host tells you that one person who will be at the party has recently returned from a trip to China. First, look at a world atlas or encyclopedia to find the major cities, then get a general idea of the geography and some basic information about the country. Or check in your local library for recent magazine or newspaper articles on China.

Many people volunteer their time and talents for special causes or organizations. If you discover that a guest volunteers his or her time for a certain charity, make a phone call to research the services or benefits that it offers the community. Ask about any recent media reports that have highlighted its achievements. Then after you meet the person, refer to the organization by saying, for example:

'Jamie told me that you help at the children's hospital. I read in the newspaper about the work that volunteers do there and I

26

found it very inspiring. What kinds of things are you doing at the hospital?'

Many of your fellow guests will probably be interested in either playing or watching sport. You can learn a lot about this popular topic by reading the sports page in your local newspaper. After you meet a 'sports nut', you could say:

'Jack told me that you're a football fan. I read that our local college has a pretty good team this year. Do you think they might have any success in the local league?'

Where to find information

Whether the guest you're interested in helps with a local adult literacy scheme or teaches martial arts, find out what you can about the topic. Use these easily accessible resources:

- Peruse the papers, weekly magazines and news programmes for related topics.
- Ask your local librarian.
- If you're on the Internet, go on-line for information about the subject.
- Refer to reference books that offer notes on a broad range of subjects.

Psych yourself up

Going to a party where everyone is a stranger can be daunting. Soon after I moved house, a neighbour invited me to a party. While I normally looked forward to meeting new people at parties, on this particular evening I felt nervous walking into a room where I knew only one person, the host. As I approached the door, I considered turning around and going home – until I saw some other guests arriving. Then it was too late to bail out, so I took half-a-dozen deep breaths and said these words to myself: 'What is the worst thing that can happen? If I don't have a good time, I can always leave. Who knows, I might meet some interesting people!'

Make the 'butterflies' in your stomach fly in formation!

Only you know how you really feel when you walk into a roomful of strangers at a party. Even if you are nervous, you can appear approachable and willing to talk. Be sure to enter the room smiling, establish eye contact, and nod. Say hello and introduce yourself to the people you meet and you'll be setting a friendly tone for conversation later.

Then find the host and present him or her with a small gift, such as a bottle of wine, chocolates or flowers. It is not how much you spend on the gift that is important, but the thought that shows you appreciate your host's hospitality. This is also a good time to ask your host if he or she needs help with any last-minute details. Believe me, your host will really appreciate your thoughtfulness even if everything is under control. And talking to your host will be a warm-up for conversations with other guests at the party.

Look for a friendly face and start a conversation

Your first mission at the party is to mix with the other guests. Do this by going to where the other guests congregate. The most common places are the food tables, kitchen or drinks table. Introduce yourself immediately to those around you and start a conversation with a light comment or easy-to-answer question. The following examples and explanations illustrate the dynamics of a typical conversation.

'Hello, I live down the road from our host. My name is . . . How do you know Jean?' (Free information and an open-ended question give both people an opportunity to establish how they know the party's host.)

'This dip is delicious. I had it once in a Greek restaurant. I think it's made with yogurt. Do you like it?' (While this closed-ended question requires only a short answer, it opens the door for more conversation based on food, cooking or restaurants.)

'I don't know a soul here apart from Jean. Are you friends with the other people here?' (This disclosure shows trust by revealing what is an uncomfortable situation for many people. It also helps

28

to establish a rapport between guests who want to meet new people and make friends.)

When it comes to starting conversations, it's not what you say, it's how you say it! Most people go to parties expecting a few questions to get the conversations going. Be sure that you are ready to answer some commonly asked questions too.

Don't be a 'potted plant' – keep circulating!

Mingling is a vital part of socializing at a party, so don't 'grow roots' or stay in one part of the room for too long. A good rule to follow at a larger party is to circulate after ten or twenty minutes of conversation. Of course, looking at your watch and saying, 'Time's up! Got to move on. Bye!' would be very rude. Remember not to end your conversation abruptly, but wait for a slight pause or other appropriate time. Say you enjoyed the chat, use the person's name, and simply say you are going to circulate a little.

Joining conversations already in progress

Now that you've had a few successful one-to-one chats, it may be time to mingle and join a group of people talking. Help! How in the world can you break into the conversation without seeming pushy or being rejected? While many shy people see this as a difficult task, it is much easier than you might think. Follow these five steps:

Step 1: Look for an open group

When I go to a party, I always search for a group of people who are having a lively conversation. These people are easy to spot because they are the ones who are smiling and having fun. Their open body language says it all: 'We are having a good time, so please join us.' These guests could be talking about books, films, television programmes, or just about anything, but the chances are that humour is a fundamental part of their exchange. I enjoy these groups because they are talking about what interests me. Moreover, I go to parties to have fun, not to solve the world's problems. You, on the other hand, may prefer to discuss more penetrating or serious issues such as philosophy, political theories or ethical values. In this case, look for an open group of people who are discussing similar topics by exchanging their ideas, feelings and opinions, but not engaging in heated debates.

Step 2: Move within communicating distance

Once you spot a receptive group, move to within four or five feet of them. Establish eye contact with the speakers; smile and show that you are interested in what they are saying. You might think that this is being a bit forward, or even nosy – and in a way it is – but that's OK. Remember, people go to parties to socialize and make new friends. Also, don't assume that the guests in the group all know one another. In fact, many have probably just met for the first time and don't even know one another's names. One warning, though: if you overhear what is obviously a personal or heated conversation, move away and look for another group to join.

Open group	Closed group
O O	X X X
O O	X X
O ←←	X X X
Enter the group from here	Look for another group to join

Step 3: Show a desire to participate

Once you have established that the group is open, clearly show your desire to participate. When one guest makes a joke, be sure to smile and laugh along with the rest of the group. When someone else makes an interesting comment, nod your head. Look for who appears to be the most friendly and open person in the group, because he or she will probably be most receptive to you.

Step 4: Ask a question or make a light comment

Now is the time for you to start talking. Simply ask a question or make a comment based on what you heard the group discussing. You might share some information or anecdote related to the topic.

Hopefully, this will encourage a response or question from someone else in the group. Short of these techniques, you can always just ask, 'Do you mind if I join you?'

Step 5: Introduce yourself to the group

Always introduce yourself to the person in the group who responded to you first, and then to the other guests. It almost never fails that the other guests will take your introduction as a cue to introduce themselves, if they haven't already. These introductions help make everyone in the group feel more comfortable. Make it a point to use the guests' names right away and refer to an earlier comment or question to restart the conversation. Take care not to talk too much, be confrontational, or make judgemental comments. Your goal is to establish rapport and have a casual and fun conversation. Keep an eye out for other guests interested in joining you. When you spot someone, open up a space for him or her and you'll make a friend immediately! Introduce yourself and the others in the group. When you use the names of the people you have just met, you'll make a big impression! When you are ready to move on, shake hands with everyone, use their names, and say, 'I have enjoyed meeting you all.'

Hint: Besides the tips in Chapter 4, these additional suggestions will help you remember the names of people in a group:

- Slow down the introductions so that you have an opportunity to concentrate on and repeat aloud each person's name.
- 'Hook' the first initials of the names into short words or abbreviations. For example, if you just met Ian, Bob and Mary, think 'IBM'.
- Take a few seconds to recall the names of the people in the group.
- If you missed the name, listen carefully for someone else in the group referring to the person by his or her name.
- When you hear the name again, repeat it to yourself and then refer to the person using his or her name.

Not all groups at a party are right for you

After you have had one successful conversation in a group, move on to another. You'll discover that some groups are easier to mix with than others and are more to your liking. If your conversation doesn't go as well as you might have wished, that's OK. Perhaps it was the topic or the people in the group. That's fine – just move on and try again. Soon you'll become quite proficient at spotting the groups at parties that are right for you.

THE TEN BIGGEST MISTAKES SHY PEOPLE MAKE IN PARTY CONVERSATION

When you avoid these common communication pitfalls, you'll boost your personal appeal and have a lot more fun at parties. The mistakes are:

1 Having a negative attitude and anticipating rejection.
2 Folding your arms and not smiling.
3 Remaining silent instead of being the first to say hello.
4 Breaking the ice with a dull question such as 'What do you do?'
5 Replying with only one-word answers without revealing additional information or topics of interest.
6 Talking too much without asking questions or listening for 'key words' or 'free information' from other people.
7 Talking too little without showing interest or enthusiasm.
8 Not introducing yourself and not using the other people's names.
9 Arguing about minor details and being a know-all.
10 Ending the conversation abruptly or on a depressing subject.

6

Holding a get-together that leaves your guests talking

Hold a get-together and shed your shy image

To a shy person, holding a party may sound terrifying, but it can be one of the best ways to build social confidence and shed a 'wallflower' image. Ironically, a person who may feel reserved at someone else's party can be outgoing when he or she is the one holding a get-together.

It's true that planning a party requires you to focus on the practical aspects, including choosing the right theme, food, music and guests. But that isn't all you need to do. Experienced party-givers agree that the secrets to a party's success rest in these elements:

- Making guests feel welcome.
- Encouraging lively conversation.
- Remaining relaxed and gracious.
- Attending to details that make guests feel pampered.
- Adding a few special touches to make your get-together memorable.

Dealing with pre-party nerves

Tonight is your get-together and your guests will be arriving soon. Although you've planned and prepared your party as if you were a professional party-giver, you still might feel nervous. Do you remember in Chapter 4 you learned to focus your attention outwards towards the people you meet and not to worry about making a fool of yourself? In addition, use these techniques to minimize any last-minute jitters:

- Find a chair and sit quietly with your eyes closed for a minute or two to gather your thoughts.

- Imagine your home filled with people having fun and enjoying one another's company.
- Look around your home and absorb the party atmosphere.
- Put on some relaxing music as you attend to the final details.
- Put yourself in a 'party frame of mind' by smiling at yourself in the mirror.
- Don't worry if everything isn't perfect. Your guests won't notice or care if the scented soap in the bathroom doesn't exactly match your hand towels.
- Adopt an easy-going attitude so that you will appear gracious and relaxed.

Three steps to make guests feel welcome

As a shy person, you know how hard it can be to attend a party – even when you know some of the other guests. As a host, you can make those first few anxious minutes a lot more comfortable by helping your guests to integrate into the party area. Follow these steps.

Step 1: Welcome your guests personally

Treat your guests as if they are the most important people in your home. Offer to take their coats or show them where they can put their things.

Step 2: Spend time with new arrivals

Bring your guests into the main party area and offer them some refreshment. Start a short conversation based on something light, such as an unusual 'nibble' you have prepared for the party or a recent amusing experience. Ask them about something important in their lives, such as 'How are the children?' or 'Are you settling into your new home?' or 'How's your tomato crop coming along? I hope it's as good as last year's.' The key point is to devote your full attention to the new guests, even if only for a few minutes. This adds a personal touch that makes them feel welcome.

Step 3: Help new arrivals to mix with other guests

Introduce your new guests to the other people at the party. The shy guests will be particularly grateful if you help them over this hurdle. Before you introduce your guests, take a moment to consider what you want to say. Keep it upbeat and brief, and avoid professional titles or potentially embarrassing information. The best introductions include a personal connection and a bit of humour. For example:

> *'Excuse me everyone, but I want to introduce you to two of my oldest and dearest friends, Ted and Sheila. We went to school together – and no, I won't say how many years ago! Ted and Sheila, this is . . .'*

> *'Bill and Carol, I'd like you to meet Diana. Diana has just moved here from Cardiff, and since all your children are at the same school, I thought that you might like to get to know each other.'*

A *few tips on introductions*: Etiquette varies, depending on the group, age and culture, but these basic rules always apply:

- Introduce men to women.
- Introduce younger people to older people.
- Introduce subordinates to superiors.
- For most informal parties, introduce guests by their first names. (You may wish to include last names for more formal or social/ business get-togethers.)
- Clearly say the name of each guest and allow an extra moment for them to greet and shake hands.
- If possible, add a few words about the people so they have an easy way to start conversations.

Encouraging entertaining conversation between guests

Along with introducing guests to one another, a good host stimulates entertaining conversation. This is where revealing your guests' interests can help other shy people feel more comfortable and enliven the party atmosphere. Helping guests to mix and mingle is easy if you keep moving through the party and introducing them to one another, particularly those who share common interests. Interject a comment or open-ended question that allows your guests to talk about their 'pet subjects' or unusual experiences. For example:

'Jean, I've been meaning to ask you about your trip to Greenland on Concorde. It sounds so exciting! What was it like there?'

'Karen, tell us that funny story about the time your children . . .'

'Richard, you use the Internet a lot. What have you found lately that's really interesting?'

Easing out of the conversation

Once you get people talking, spend a few minutes enjoying their company and conversation. You can then gracefully slip out of the conversation by saying:

'Well, I can see you all have lots to talk about. Excuse me while I check on the food.'

'I can hear some new guests arriving. Excuse me for a moment.'

'Don't mind me. I need to slip away to ask someone something.'

Keep an eye out for 'difficult' guests

As you move through the party and chat with your friends, keep your eyes open for anyone having a problem with a 'difficult' guest. It could be two people arguing, a bore trapping another guest in a corner, or someone who is drinking too much. In any case, one guest's inappropriate behaviour can make the rest of your guests feel embarrassed and uncomfortable. As the host, you're the one your guests will look to to rectify the situation. The following 'conversational crisis management' techniques can help to keep difficult guests from spoiling your party.

Defusing an argument
Discussing and exchanging different opinions at parties can be stimulating and entertaining, but some people (particularly if they have had too much to drink) may forget that arguments are inappropriate. If you hear a discussion heating up to the critical

point, don't wait until tempers boil over. Quickly step in to calm everyone down and change the topic. Believe me, the guests will thank you for saving everyone from an embarrassing scene. To tactfully defuse the situation, use the guests' names and say something like:

> *'Les. Mick. Hang on a second. I think this discussion is getting a bit too intense. After all, this is a party – not a war tribunal. Let's change the subject to something a little lighter. Les, I understand your son's soccer team is playing in a championship match next week.'*

> *'Gail. Tim. I'm calling a halt on this discussion. I know you're both very passionate about this subject, but I'd really appreciate it if you would just agree to disagree – at least for tonight. Tim, are you planning any trips in your campervan this summer?'*

Rescuing a guest from a bore

Everyone knows the uncomfortable feeling of being trapped by the tedious person who reveals the endings of books and films, tells long-winded stories, discusses his or her latest illness, or pumps other guests for free professional advice. As the host, it's your job to rescue a guest from a bore's clutches. Here is how you can do it gracefully:

> *'Sorry to interrupt you two, but I need Steve's help for something. He'll be back in a few minutes.'* (Then the rescued person can get 'conveniently distracted' by another guest.)

> *'Phil, sorry to interrupt you and Beth, but I want to introduce you both to some people. They're over here. Come on.'* (Introducing the bore and trapped guest into a larger group makes it more difficult for a blabbermouth to monopolize the conversation. Plus, the now-freed guest can excuse himself or herself more easily from the conversation.)

> *'Fred, do you mind if I steal Jane away from you? I need her help in the kitchen, RIGHT NOW! Jane, it's time for you to heat up those wonderful-looking vol-au-vents that you brought.'* (Asking the bore for assistance allows the trapped guest to escape.)

A final tip on dealing with difficult guests: An assertive approach is best when confronting a guest who engages in any kind of inappropriate behaviour. Be friendly but firm. Ask to speak with the person privately in another room. Then briefly define the problem behaviour and ask him or her to stop.

Holding a party is fun and a great confidence builder

It takes a lot of work and planning to hold a party, but the pay-offs are worth it! Your creativity and sense of fun will enliven your get-together. Your guests will have a great time and will see you as a caring and outgoing person who knows how to entertain at home. Helping your guests mix and knowing that you can handle any unexpected problems that may arise will boost your confidence tenfold. You may still be a little reserved at other people's parties, but as the host in your own home, you will shine all evening.

FIFTEEN TIPS FOR ENJOYING YOUR OWN PARTIES

1 The more you prepare ahead of time, the more you will enjoy your party.
2 Consider a theme. It livens parties up and gives the guests something to talk about.
3 Guests are the most important part of any get-together. The more diverse the group, the greater the opportunities for spontaneity and fun.
4 Invite people who you think will mix well together.
5 Let your guests know the arrival time, proper attire, what to bring and, if necessary, the time you are sitting down to eat.
6 Pay equal attention to all your guests.
7 Always have more than enough food and refreshments on hand.
8 Distribute food in various locations so guests can circulate, nibble and talk.
9 Add an extra touch of class with flowers, candles and scented soaps.
10 Have a variety of music, including dance and easy listening.
11 Be flexible and prepared for the unexpected spill or broken wineglass.
12 Once the doorbell starts ringing, stop preparing and enjoy your guests' company.
13 Don't engage in frantic or nervous clean-up until after the party.
14 When everyone has left, have a drink with a friend and toast to a wonderful night of fun and entertaining.
15 Relax, smile, and have a great time. After all, it's your party!

7

Talking your way out of 'toxic conversations'

Beware of conversational traps!

Do you remember the last time you attended a party, family gathering or business meeting and got trapped into what could be called a 'toxic conversation'? The awkward situation probably started innocently enough as a 'friendly exchange of ideas'. Then, with lightning speed, a barrage of stinging words or personal comments caught you off guard. You thought that a brusque retort would put an end to it, but that only encouraged the loudmouthed person even more. By the time you realized that you had 'taken the bait', the aggressive lout had sprung his conversational trap and delivered the verbal coup de grâce. You languished in public humiliation while the boor gloated over his triumph and your embarrassment. The question is, 'How can you avoid becoming a victim of a conversational bully and escape a toxic conversation with your self-esteem intact?'

Don't overreact – do stay calm

If you find your conversation heading for a confrontation or argument, keep your cool so you can find a way to change the topic. Remaining calm shows confidence, and it gives you time to think of an appropriate response. The biggest mistake you can make in responding to a personal attack or unfair criticism is to 'shoot back with both barrels'. Fighting back verbally shows the other person that he or she has hit a nerve, and now you are in for a real battle. Once an aggressive person identifies a vulnerable spot, he or she will keep picking at it until you give in or lose your temper. On the other hand, if you don't react to a provocation, you offer nothing for the conversational shark to feed on.

Don't argue – do listen

Shy people are particularly attractive targets for conversational bullies who like to draw unsuspecting individuals into a verbal fray.

Remember, bullies love to argue and win because it makes them feel more important when they dominate others. If someone challenges you, don't react. Instead, hold your ground and ask an open-ended question. This stalling strategy gives you time to develop a response that allows you to find an exit. The following examples show how to stand up to a verbal bully and deflect a personal attack without getting sucked into an argument.

Quarrelsome boor: *'It is people like you who are ruining our country!'*

Shy person: *'Excuse me?* (Looking surprised) *Are you talking to me?'*

Quarrelsome boor: *'You're damn right I'm talking to you!* (Wagging a finger in your face and getting louder) *You and your disgusting people have really made a mess of our country and it's about time we respectable people did something about it!'*

Shy person (in a calm, firm voice): *'I agree, our country has problems, but I'm not sure exactly what you are talking about. Could you be more specific?'*

Quarrelsome boor (getting worked up and moving closer): *'You know exactly what I mean! You ought to be ashamed of yourself!'* (Casting the bait)

Shy person (ignoring the insult and in a cool, confident voice): *'Actually, I still have no idea what you are talking about.* (Frustrating the boor by not taking the bait and forcing him to start over again) *What are you trying to say?'*

Quarrelsome boor (reaching boiling point with no one to fight with, he pulls out all the stops): *'You [blankity blank-blank] people always play the innocent, but you know damn well what's the matter with this country, and you're it! Why, if it were up to me, I'd . . .'*

Again, don't respond to the attack, no matter how tempted you may be. Displaying a cool aloofness shows you are in control and that you are not going to fall into his or her trap. Conversational boors usually give up and look for someone else to harass when their provocation fails to get reactions. If, however, the boor persists, then excusing yourself from the conversation is perfectly acceptable.

> Shy person (acknowledging the boor's irate behaviour and setting the stage for a polite exit): *'I'm sure you have your reasons for getting so upset, but I still don't understand what you are trying to say. If you'll excuse me, there's someone else I'd like to say hello to. Goodbye.'*

'Let's agree to disagree'

Fortunately, not every discussion of opinion ends in an argument. When there is a mutual exchange of ideas, many people enjoy broadening their understanding of an issue. However, when debating emotionally charged issues, you and someone else with vastly different values or opinions will probably never agree. If left unchecked, this volatile situation can escalate into a toxic conversation that can permanently damage a relationship.

For example, you may support your local MP whom your conversational partner despises. Both of you know that neither of you will change your opinions. In fact, the more you argue, the more tightly you will cling to your individual positions. However, you can show you are listening and understand the key factors influencing the other person's viewpoint while clearly exercising your right to disagree. These examples show you how to politely disagree:

> *'I understand that you think our local economy is going down the drain because of the plant closures. Nevertheless, I also see small businesses expanding into other areas that will make our towns less dependent on one large employer, and I think that is good.'*

> *'From what you say, it's clear that you don't think our town has a bright future, but I can't think of anywhere else I'd rather live.'*

Change the topic before emotions escalate out of control

To avoid saying something that both of you will later regret, you can redirect the conversation to a less inflammatory topic. Don't wait until emotions and voices reach fever pitch to end the discussion. In a firm and friendly voice say, 'Since we're not going to change each other's minds, let's just agree to disagree. By the way, how is your vegetable allotment coming along this year?'

Dodging unwanted questions

Since you have a right to privacy, you are under no obligation to provide an answer just because a busybody asks you a personal question about your finances, political persuasion, family matters or health. To discuss or not to discuss, and how much to reveal, is your choice. Never reveal information that you prefer to keep private. Use these techniques to evade nosy inquisitors and avoid toxic topics.

Technique 1: Provide a vague answer and ask a question

This technique deflects unwanted questions with answers that provide little or no specific information. Asking a question in return throws the conversational ball into the other person's court.

For example, if a nosy in-law asks: *'How much do you earn?'*
You can say: *'I earn enough to keep me happy. How are you getting by in these tough times?'*

If an office gossip asks: *'Is it all true what they say about your new boss?'*
You can say: *'My new boss and I get along very well. How is your part of the project coming along?'*

Technique 2: Refuse to answer and change the subject

This technique suggests that the question is unwelcome and that you are not going to answer it. Changing the subject offers both people a diplomatic way out of a sensitive situation.

For example, if a nosy boss asks: *'What do you do all weekend by yourself?'*
You can say: *'I prefer to keep my personal life private. When do you want the Jones file?'*

If a competitive colleague asks: *'How much was your pay rise?'*

You can say: *'I'd rather not say. By the way, how's your job search going?'*

Technique 3: Refuse to answer and discourage more questions

This technique makes it absolutely clear that the question is 'out of bounds'. A follow-up word or two helps discourage persistent or aggressive people who may try to take advantage of a personal relationship to gain private information.

For example, if a competitor asks: *'What has XYZ Inc. invested in recently that I won't read about in the papers?'*
You can say: *'Please don't ask me questions like that. My clients' financial investments are confidential.'*

If a meddling friend asks: *'So what did Sally tell you that was so hush-hush?'*
You can say: *'You know I don't tell my friends' secrets. That's why you and I are still friends.'*

Make silence work for you

Dealing with confrontations and toxic topics is not always easy, and pushy people can drive you to breaking point. Whenever that happens, pause for a moment, take a deep breath, and say nothing. A short period of silence can defuse nosy or aggressive people because they will not know what to do when you do not react to their taunts. Then, when you are ready, respond in a way that maintains your integrity, self-respect and, above all, composure. When silence is the appropriate response, follow this advice: *no reply is best.*

EIGHT TIPS FOR AVOIDING TOXIC CONVERSATIONS

1 Stay cool and never let conversational bullies make you lose your temper.
2 Don't feel that you have to defend yourself or respond to accusations.
3 Change the topic before you get trapped into an argument.
4 Ignore nasty comments or verbal attacks – it drives bullies crazy!
5 Use your sense of humour to defuse a political argument.
6 Avoid people who like to play 'devil's advocate'. They are just looking for victims.
7 Never go on the attack in a toxic conversation.
8 Get away from toxic conversationalists as quickly as possible.

8

Proposing a toast to friends and family

'We want you to propose a toast'

Oh no! At the last minute your best friends ask you to propose a toast at their wedding reception. They know that you're shy, but do they realize that you would rather have a tooth out without an anaesthetic injection than stand up and speak before a group? You can't insult them by saying no, so you reluctantly accept the honour. The only problem is, you have no idea what to say and the big day is tomorrow! What are you going to do?

Good toasts make joyous occasions even more special

You can do one of three things when you propose a toast at a special event such as a wedding reception, birthday or anniversary party. First, you can mumble a few benign words that fall flat as a pancake. Second, you can 'wing it', risking an inappropriate comment or slip of the tongue that will embarrass everyone – and especially you! Or third, you can impress everyone with a few choice words that will enhance the special occasion. If you want your words to remain in everyone's hearts and minds – and have fun, too – follow these steps to prepare, practise and propose your toast.

Step 1: Identify the audience

As in all public speaking, knowing your audience and the environment in which you are going to speak increases your confidence and helps you decide what to say. To that end, find out the following information:

- Who will be present? (This information helps you choose appropriate quotations and anecdotes for your toast.)
- Is it an intimate celebration or a large formal affair? (Informal and personal toasts are welcome for small family celebrations. A traditional toast works better for a larger, more formal occasion.)
- Is the event being held inside or outside? (If the event is going to

be outside, you may have to practise your toast at a louder volume so that everyone can hear your 'pearls of wisdom'.)

- Will you need a microphone? (If you don't test the microphone before proposing your toast, it will undoubtedly fail or will squeal so loudly that it will blow the ears, hats and toupees off the guests.)
- Who else is proposing toasts and when is your turn? (Knowing your position in the line-up of toasts gives you an opportunity to mentally prepare for your big moment.)

Step 2: Choose words that show acknowledgement and appreciation

For shy people, the good news about speaking before a group is that the best toasts are short, simple, warm and personal. Toasts can be funny or heartwarming, and are always optimistic. Start by consulting the many excellent quotation books that are now available. You can also find inspiring lines at your nearest greeting card shop and even inscribed (not painted!) on the walls of libraries and public buildings. Draw on your favourite films, television programmes, poems, novels, and even badges with printed slogans for poignant words that put a little 'spice' in your toast. Usually, though, the best source of inspiration is your personal experiences with the person or people you are honouring.

Step 3: Write out and practise your toast

Shy people take note! Professional speakers know the importance of the first few moments of a speech, so they write, memorize and practise their opening lines until they can say them flawlessly. Adlibbing or failing to practise a toast, especially If you are inexperienced, have had a little too much to drink, or are nervous, can lead to an embarrassing moment. Consider the husband who made this unfortunate slip of the tongue. After one too many glasses of champagne, he toasted his wife at their fiftieth wedding anniversary party by saying, 'Here's to my petty wife!' Oops! Obviously, he meant to say 'pretty', but no matter how much he apologized, the damage was done. The moral of the story is to know what you are going to say and rehearse it aloud at least five minutes before you propose your toast. You won't be sorry.

A few words of caution: Always anticipate how individual audience members might react to your words *before* you say them. If you are not sure your words are appropriate, they probably are not. *If you have any doubt, leave those questionable words out!*

Step 4: Make a last-minute check

The big day has arrived and your time to speak is a few minutes away. You have chosen your words with care and have practised your delivery. Although you're still a little nervous, conscientious preparation increases your confidence and poise. Now is the time to do a last-minute check.

- Silently rehearse your toast, focusing especially on the first and last sentences.
- About fifteen minutes before you speak, make a short trip to the rest room to check your appearance, gather your thoughts, and practise your toast again.
- Make funny faces in the mirror and blow air through closed lips to relax your jaws.
- Make clenched fists and then open your hands to help you relax your muscles.
- Take a drink of warm water and quietly clear your throat.
- Take a few deep breaths to calm your jitters, return to the group, and wait for your turn.
- When you receive your cue, stand up, pause for a few seconds to plant your feet, smile, and then look at your audience.
- Gaze with admiration at the person or people you are about to toast.
- Speak loudly enough so that everyone can hear.
- After the toast, nod to and smile at your audience before you sit down.

Toasts for anniversaries, engagements and weddings

Happy memories and an optimism about the future are the key ideas to focus on for these joyous occasions. Begin a wedding anniversary toast by taking a trip down memory lane. Make the past come alive by using words that describe the music, films or events that reflect the couple's experiences. Then forecast a rosy and rewarding future. If appropriate, you can adapt a humorous quotation to fit an engagement toast.

Proposing a birthday toast

Birthday toasts are simple and fun. The main points to emphasize in the toast are gratitude, affection, friendship, good health and the future. One easy way to personalize your toast is to describe some significant events in the year of the person's birth based on his or her interests. Then use words related to this interest to show your appreciation. You can use almanacs, encyclopedias and special-interest books to find fun facts about practically any subject or hobby.

Toasting family and friends

Reunions, parties and celebration dinners frequently call for toasts. Use words like *lasting friendships*, *loyalty*, *fond memories*, *togetherness* and *good times together*. Talk about *humorous times*, *unforgettable experiences* and *tender moments*. These words describe the stuff of close relationships. Avoid any mention of past arguments or disagreements. Then wish everyone many more happy times together.

A toast to family members often focuses on appreciation and personal challenges. You can also use gentle humour to poke a little fun at parents, siblings and relatives.

Toasts make your relationship special

Proposing a toast at a birthday, wedding or family get-together is an honour that even a shy person like you can enjoy. When you take the time to choose, practise and present the right words for a toast, everyone will see you as a confident speaker. But even more important, your friends and family will cherish your words long after the celebration is over.

THE FLIP SIDE OF A TOAST: A GRACEFUL RESPONSE

Follow these dos and don'ts when *you* are the person being toasted:

Do:

✓ Remain seated with your hands folded in your lap or on the table.
✓ Say 'Thank you' and, if you wish, add a few words of appreciation.
✓ Wish everyone the same happiness that they wish for you.
✓ Drink only after others have finished toasting you.

Don't:

✗ Drink to yourself.
✗ Pick up your glass until the toast is over.
✗ Feign modesty by claiming unworthiness.
✗ Recite a tedious list of people you want to thank.

9

'Telebonding' your way to personal relationships

'Telebonding' helps build new relationships

Telebonding is the process of developing, nurturing and enhancing new and close relationships via the telephone. Perhaps you met someone on holiday or at a conference whom you would like to get to know better. The bad news is that you and the other person live in different parts of the country. The good news is that you exchanged phone numbers and that there is a real possibility of establishing and maintaining a long-distance relationship.

Even if you are shy, you can initiate a new telebonding relationship by phoning the other person. It is helpful to have a 'reason' for the call and then build the conversation around that subject area.

Take care not to chat for too long or, on the other hand, to cut your conversation short: about ten to twenty minutes on your first call is sufficient. If the other person responds enthusiastically to your call, you can say, 'I enjoyed talking to you. Would you mind if I rang you again?' If the answer is yes, you have started the telebonding process. Admittedly, it takes some nerve for a shy person like you to ring a stranger you've only met once or twice, but think of what you have to gain.

Telebonding helps maintain and nurture established friendships

Do you have an old friend who lives halfway across the country whom you see only once a year, at best? Why let the distance keep you apart? Don't be shy about frequent phoning. Telebonding allows you to maintain existing relationships that otherwise might whither and die. For example, my wife and one of her college friends rarely see each other, but have had weekly phone conversations for years. Their friendship continues to grow and they are even closer now than they were 25 years ago. When they do see each other, it is as if they have been talking face-to-face all the time they were apart. This is telebonding at its best!

Telebonding helps bring family members closer together

Did you move away from home and over the years lose touch with your parents, siblings or other relatives? Telebonding is an ideal way to re-establish family ties and build stronger personal bonds. For example, when I moved away from home, my sister and I rarely rang each other. Although we enjoyed the time we spent together during the Christmas holidays, the only other time we spoke during the year was for our obligatory birthday phone calls. After several years of this pattern of communication, I noticed our relationship was becoming more distant. Then my sister and her husband suggested that my wife and I join them on holiday. As the frequency of our phone calls increased, so did the quality of our relationship. Now we talk at least once or twice a month! Once again, telebonding enhances a personal relationship that was in danger of disappearing.

Telebonding is a way to re-establish old friendships

If you haven't rung a friend or family member for a while, the conversation may take a little extra time to get going. The exchange may feel awkward at first, especially if there are short periods of silence. You may feel tongue-tied and want to hang up, but stay cool and keep on talking.

To feed the conversation, ask easy-to-answer open-ended questions and listen for key words, free information and implied statements. As the other person speaks, listen for the topics that he or she seems to want to talk about. At the same time, be sure to share plenty of free information of your own so the other person will know what you want to talk about.

Telephone etiquette

There are right and wrong ways to talk on the phone. The following ten tips for telephone etiquette will enhance telebonding with your conversational partner and help you overcome your initial shyness.

Tip 1: *Always identify yourself when you phone someone*

As unbelievable as it may sound, there are some adults who still play the childish telephone games 'Can you guess who this is?' My usual response to this lame way to start a phone conversation is a simple 'No, should I?' If that poor excuse for a telephone introduction isn't maddening enough, some people launch into a long story the moment the other party answers the telephone. Most people need a few moments to recognize even the most familiar voice on the phone when a call comes unexpectedly.

Tip 2: *Ask whether you're phoning at a convenient time*

Many people think that an unannounced visit to a friend is considered rude, yet many people do just that when they phone and assume that the person they are ringing is available to talk. Many people don't even consider that their phone call may come at an inconvenient time. That is why it is important to understand that the telephone is the 'electronic doorway' to the home. Whether the person you are calling is a new friend or family member, it is good manners to ask, 'Is this a good time to talk?' Or 'Have I phoned you in the middle of dinner (a meeting, another phone call, feeding the baby, etc.)?' This gives the person you are ringing an option to talk now or return your call at a more convenient time. If he or she is busy or unavailable, simply ask, 'When would be a good time to get back to you?'

How to say 'Now is not a good time for me to talk'

If you are shy, you may feel reluctant to tell a friend or acquaintance that he or she is ringing at an inconvenient time. It is perfectly all right to say, 'Bill, I'd love to talk to you, but I'm right in the middle of dinner (just getting ready to go out, watching my favourite television programme, etc.). Can I get back to you in about an hour or so?' Then it is up to you to return the call when it is convenient. If this is an acquaintance, you may want to say, 'By the way, remind me of your phone number again.'

Tip 3: *Avoid screening your phone calls*

Many shy people with answering machines now screen their calls before answering the phone to avoid inconvenient interruptions or unsolicited sales calls from double glazing firms or companies selling time share holidays. If, however, you *always* screen your calls, it can give the impression that you are unavailable, antisocial or uncomfortable talking on the phone. Answer your phone unless you have a good reason not to, such as when you are working, eating or sleeping.

Tip 4: Don't keep two people on the line

Call Waiting is a service that allows you to receive a second call while you are already speaking to someone on the phone. However, Call Waiting can cause offence if you put the first person on hold while you talk to the second caller.

Here is a good rule to follow if you receive a second call: put the first call on hold for no more than 45 seconds. Any longer than that is just plain rude. You can say to the second caller, 'I'm on the other line right now. Let me get back to you in a few minutes or . . .' However, if it is vital that you take the second call, then quickly go back to your first caller and say something like 'I'm sorry to cut you off, but I need to take this call. Can I ring you back in about an hour?'

Tip 5: Don't just complain about your problems

When you ring a friend, you might want to talk at length about your problems. While venting some frustrations during a phone conversation with a friend is OK, going on too long can inhibit telebonding and put a strain on the relationship.

After complaining about your difficult boss, irritating neighbour or prying in-law, share some positive experiences as well. Change the conversation by saying something like 'Well, I suppose I've been grumbling about my . . . long enough. By the way, I forgot to tell you that I've signed up for a course that's been given on the Internet.' Or shift the conversation to your friend by asking, 'What's new with you?'

Tip 6: Ask about events in the other person's life

Shy people often hesitate to ask questions because they don't want to appear nosy or too personal. Ironically, friends get offended when you *don't* ask them questions about the major experiences in their lives. The reasons are simple: friends like to talk about themselves, and they usually want to share intimate details with those they trust. This is what telebonding is all about.

Show interest by asking the other person about the important events in his or her life. This shows that you care and helps to build rapport and trust.

Tip 7: Don't criticize or make judgemental statements

When your friend complains endlessly, you may feel like saying, 'Stop whingeing, you wimp!' or 'If you had listened to me in the first place you wouldn't be in this mess!' The tendency to criticize and make harsh comments about a friend's behaviour, predicaments or decisions – even if they are well intentioned – can inhibit telebonding and damage a relationship.

Avoid offering advice unless someone asks for it. Then, present your words of wisdom sparingly and tactfully. Consider posing questions such as 'What are your options?' or 'In a perfect world, what would you do?' The point here is not to advise, but to be a good listener and help your friend find his or her own solutions.

Tip 8: Avoid dwelling on negative topics

Unhappy personal relationships, complicated economic theories, or a rehash of the world's problems are legitimate topics of conversation, but when discussions get bogged down in these heavy topics for too long, it can become a bit too depressing. And if you are guilty of dwelling on negative topics, the other person may feel trapped and not be too enthusiastic about your next phone call.

Provide some light relief by using your sense of humour to show you can keep these issues in perspective. The best telebonding occurs when both people can share a laugh with each other. Change the topic of conversation to something that both of you feel good about.

Tip 9: End your conversation on a positive note

As in face-to-face conversations, if you end your phone contact without warning or on a negative note, it leaves the other person feeling uncomfortable. When this happens, he or she may feel less inclined to talk to you the next time you ring. Telebonding increases when you find some aspect of the conversation that you can rephrase in a positive way. Repeat what you liked about the exchange and conclude your phone conversation in a warm and enthusiastic way.

Tip 10: Initiate your share of the phone calls

Good relationships are based on give-and-take, and telebonding is no different. If you always wait for your friend or family member to ring you, then you may be giving the impression that the contact is not that important to you. On the other hand, if you are the one who always makes the phone call, then you might be the one who feels slighted. If the cost of long-distance phone calls is an issue, then discuss it openly. There are various schemes and cheap-rate periods for long-distance calls that can make telebonding quite economical. Besides, if you lived in the same town and went out to lunch with your friend once a week, you would probably spend far more than the cost of a long-distance call. What is more important is that each party in a long-distance relationship makes their fair share of the phone calls. When this happens, the telephone can enhance your relationships.

Telebonding builds relationships across the road, city or country

Most shy people want more contact with the people they care about because it makes them feel good and fulfils a need for intimacy. Whether you want to develop a long-distance romance, chat with an old friend, or build bonds with a family member, telebonding will improve your ability to communicate. The next time you want to share some good news or just have a conversation to discuss the latest news, ring a friend and watch your relationship grow.

THE TEN BIGGEST MISTAKES IN TELEPHONE ETIQUETTE

Taking telephone communication for granted can lead to embarrassing moments and hurt feelings. Avoid these common mistakes and your telephone relationships will increase.

1 Not identifying yourself when you ring.
2 Assuming you are ringing at a convenient time.
3 Constantly screening your phone calls.
4 Keeping two people on the line at once.
5 Only talking about your problems.
6 Not asking about the important events in other people's lives.
7 Criticizing or making judgemental statements.
8 Dwelling on depressing subjects.
9 Ending your conversation abruptly.
10 Not ringing on a regular basis.

Part 3 Speaking in business situations

10

Being interviewed for a new job

Write your own script

Today is the day of that all-important job interview and you don't want to say the wrong thing or get tongue-tied. You are hopeful because you have an impressive CV and lots of experience, but when you enter the company's office, you discover that three other applicants are also being interviewed for the position. How is the interviewer going to decide who gets the job? The fact is that good CVs only get you the interview, not the job. Your demeanour plays a vital role when you sell yourself and your skills to the interviewer. If he or she stereotypes you as 'shy' then you might as well kiss goodbye your chances of getting the job!

Avoid being stereotyped as shy – be ready with a prepared introduction

Studies show that you have less than five minutes to make a positive and memorable impression on the interviewer, so you need to know what you are going to say. When shy people get nervous, they typically clam up or ramble on about where they went to school and what jobs they have had.

To avoid these pitfalls, give a concise introduction that tells the interviewer three of the most important points about you. Explain clearly how your skills can benefit the company and save them money.

Communicating confidence is your competitive edge

Do you exude confidence or do you let your shyness show when you are interviewed for a job? Can you clearly answer questions or do you fumble for the right words? Most people do not include the ability to express themselves clearly on their CV. However, your communication savvy can convince an interviewer that you are the right person for the job.

The interviewer has many questions about your abilities, experience and communication skills. Can you clearly describe and back up your proposals? How do you react under pressure? Do you shy away from or embrace competition? Are you someone who works well in a team? Can you skilfully deal with difficult clients and colleagues? The way you conduct yourself during the interview will help you to answer these questions and give your interviewer valuable insight into your abilities. In other words, communication skills help to show that you are up to the job.

Open body language shows poise

Shy people often unconsciously reveal a lack of confidence through their closed body language. Never forget that it is not just what you say, it is how you say it. Walk confidently; keep your head up, make friendly eye contact, smile, and offer to shake hands as you enter the interviewer's office. After you sit down, lean forward slightly in your chair and wait for the interview to begin. Be aware that the interviewer is probably observing your body language during the short period of silence while 'looking over' your CV. Keep your body language open, with your arms unfolded and your hands away from your face. Now is a good time to mentally review the points you want to make about yourself and the questions you want to ask during the interview. Once the interview begins, you may periodically 'mirror' the interviewer's open body language. This will help build rapport between you.

Your persuasive voice: moderate volume + enthusiasm = confidence

Do you remember the last time you were at a job interview and the interviewer asked you to repeat your answers because you were speaking too softly? Nothing reveals nervousness more than a soft, quivering voice or monotone. Along with your body language, the tone of your voice reveals a great deal about your confidence and is a powerful selling tool. When you introduce yourself, speak in a moderate volume and with plenty of enthusiasm. Enunciate your words and use the tone of your voice to emphasize the words that you want the interviewer to remember most. Before your interview, prepare at home: use a tape recorder to practise your prepared introduction and build your vocal confidence. Or practise introducing yourself to a friend or family member. Remember that practice will make you feel more confident and comfortable during your interview.

Communicate your abilities and achievements

Shy people often refrain from talking too much about themselves, but a job interview is no time to be modest. To be seriously considered for a position, you need to express your achievements in an unaffected and straightforward way. No one will know just how good you really are at what you do unless you tell them. A glowing testimonial letter or two from a past client or employer doesn't hurt either. In other words, it is OK to gently 'blow your own trumpet', as you learned in Chapter 2. Do not hesitate to state your accomplishments and their benefits to past employers without exaggerating their impact. If the interviewer is unfamiliar with the technical aspects of your previous jobs, use familiar words instead of abbreviations, acronyms or jargon, and resist the temptation to go into complicated explanations.

Ask questions to uncover an employer's needs

Why should an employer give you a job? Just because you are an attractive person and competent is not a good enough reason. You must emphasize that the employer or business will benefit by employing you. To sell yourself, you need to discover the employer's specific needs. Then, and only then, can you convince the interviewer that you are the right person to fill the position.

Exactly how do you find out what the employer needs? Simple. Ask questions. Use the local library, chamber of commerce or newspapers to research the industry as a whole, and in prticular the company for which you are being interviewed. Then ask informed questions that incorporate the information you have unearthed. Not only does this demonstrate that you know something about the company, but it also persuades the interviewer that you are confident and well-informed.

Asking questions allows you to indicate your interest in the company, cover points that the interviewer doesn't bring up, and display knowledge of the industry as a whole.

Explain how your skills can benefit the employer

How will an employer benefit from giving you this job? You must be able to answer this question, even if the interviewer doesn't ask it directly. If you dwell on long detailed explanations without highlighting how your skills will benefit the interviewer's company, then you will be communicating only half the message. Shy people who work as professional engineers, accountants, lawyers, computer engineers and scientists, and in other technically oriented positions, frequently make this mistake during job interviews.

For example, during a job interview, an exceedingly bright but shy computer engineer explained the features of a particular software program at great length. Finally, the interviewer interrupted to ask, 'It's obvious that you know a lot about computers, but how can you help our company to increase its profit?' To you, the value of your skills may seem obvious, but do not assume others share your perspective or understanding. Tell them what you can do and how they will benefit.

Handling embarrassing and trick questions

'So why *exactly* were you sacked from your last job?' is the kind of stressful question that can leave anyone – especially a shy person – flustered and tongue-tied. The trick to dealing with stressful questions is to anticipate them and prepare your answers ahead of time. Expect questions relating to your on-the-job performance, but don't feel that you must answer illegal or inappropriate questions about your health, family or other personal issues. While most interviewers ask legitimate questions to assess your skills, some may make improper inquiries or set verbal traps to see how you respond under pressure. If an interviewer asks you negative or hostile questions, be ready to reply with a positive statement about yourself. Never repeat negative statements. In your reply, be sure to include extra information that reinforces your special strengths whenever possible.

64

Be prepared for stressful questions, inappropriate questions or even illegal questions, but remember that your goal is to move on in the interviewing process and get a job offer – not alienate the interviewer with an angry response.

Make sure you don't 'ring any alarm bells'

Some shy people may mistake an interviewer's inquisitiveness as a signal to 'reveal all' about an unpleasant employment experience. Tempting as it may be, avoid negative comments about past bosses, colleagues or employers. Negative comments 'ring alarm bells' for interviewers and may suggest that you find it difficult to work with others.

Questions to ask about the position and salary

Shy people often forget that they have a perfect right to ask the interviewer certain questions about the jobs they seek and company policies. In fact, you are interviewing them as much as they're interviewing you! Preparing a list of questions will build your confidence for when you reach this point in the interview. What do you want to know about the job you are being interviewed for? Think this through beforehand, and ask any questions that the interviewer didn't cover.

Sum up what you have to offer

End your interview the same way that you began it. Tell the interviewer the three most important things you want him or her to remember about you. Sell yourself as a congenial, skilled professional who meets deadlines and works within budgets. Emphasize that you are flexible, can consistently produce desired results on time, and work well with others. In addition, align your goals with those of the company. Remember that the only reason an interviewer will even consider employing you for a job is because you've convinced him or her of your capacity to help the business succeed in its financial goals or mission.

Conclude by actually asking for the job

The interview is nearly over and you have given it your best shot. You have confidently summarized how you can benefit the company. You have answered the interviewer's questions clearly and candidly. Now is the time to thank the interviewer for the opportunity to talk about yourself; then you should do one more thing: ask for the job.

To a shy person like you, it may sound pushy, but every successful salesperson knows that to get the sale you need to ask for it. Since you are selling *yourself*, the best way to emphasize that you want the job is simply ask for it!

11

Leading a meeting with confidence

'You want me to lead the meeting!?'

Oh no! Your boss has just asked you – the shyest person in your office – to organize and present the department's weekly staff meeting. As you imagine yourself before an audience of your peers, subordinates and supervisors, your stomach does a double back somersault. How are you going to keep your knees from knocking and your voice from quivering? What are you going to say, and how in the world are you going to handle some of those wild characters in your department who love to give the person taking the meeting a hard time?

Standing in front of your colleagues and taking charge can be frightening, but if you know how to handle it, taking a meeting can build your confidence and give your career a big boost. Even if you are shy, you can impress your peers, subordinates and supervisors if you know the three secrets to leading a productive meeting: being well organized, sticking to your agenda and timetable, and keeping control of the group. The following ten rules for better meetings will help you to take a meeting with confidence.

Ten confidence-boosting rules for better meetings

Rule 1: Set your objectives
Clearly defining four or five objectives for your meeting builds self-confidence because it clarifies your goals, thus making them easier to achieve.

Rule 2: Prepare a written agenda and timetable
When you know your objectives and roughly how long it will take to accomplish each one, you are in control of the meeting. By preparing a written agenda with a minute-by-minute timetable, you can judge if your meeting goals are reasonable within the allotted time. If you conclude that the agenda is unrealistic or too pressurized, then make

your schedule adjustments before the meeting. Covering a few important meeting objectives thoroughly is more productive than speeding through six or seven major issues with only cursory comments. The more meetings you take, the more confident and skilled you will become at estimating how long various issues will take to cover.

To show others that you are well prepared, distribute the agenda a few days before the meeting. This informs people of the meeting's purpose, gives them time to prepare, and allows them to plan their other tasks around it. While flexibility in running the meeting is essential, sticking with your agenda and timetable shows you are well organized and is an important confidence-booster.

Rule 3: Invite the right people

'Not another boring meeting!' is often the cry of people who do not belong at a meeting in the first place. What could undermine your self-confidence more than forcing everyone in a department to attend a meeting where only a handful participate? Instead, boost your credibility by inviting only the people who need to attend the meeting and can make some contributions. You can always send a memo or e-mail to the people who did not need to attend but need to know the results. Then create an eye-catching memo about the meeting for distribution to the attendees.

Rule 4: Allow people time to prepare for brainstorming sessions

Inexperienced meeting leaders often ask for ideas from attendees without having given them adequate time to prepare. If they are in the least bit shy, their typical responses will be blank stares and precious few ideas – and a diminishing image of you as a leader. As in all forms of public speaking, preparation makes the difference when calling upon people for their ideas or comments.

If your objective is to solicit input from each attendee then tell them about the meeting at least a week ahead. Make sure that each person knows what to expect and that you want him or her to speak. This sets clear expectations and gives the attendees enough preparation time to think about what they want to say. You'll get the desired results when you allow them to formulate their comments before presenting them to even a small group in an informal setting. Short, zippy memos describing all the pertinent details can save lots of time, set the tone for the meeting, and encourage shy attendees to participate more.

Rule 5: Check the room and electronic equipment before the meeting

Have you ever gone into a meeting to find that there were not enough chairs and that you had to lean against the wall or sit on the floor for over an hour? Or have you been in a meeting where the room was so cold that your teeth chattered, or so stuffy that you nearly fell asleep? The worst-case scenario is when you thought your company's product demonstration video cassette was loaded in the video recorder, and when you turned it on, attendees saw your brother-in-law's bachelor party home video. Oops! Nothing can sap your confidence and ruin your meeting faster than ignoring the important logistical details that support your meeting's objectives.

Be aware that the physical environment in which you hold a meeting and the audiovisual equipment you use will affect your presentation and credibility. Therefore, make sure that the room's temperature, seating and lighting are comfortable. Depending on the time of your meeting, you may also want to provide coffee, water, and maybe some food to nibble on.

Always, always, always check audiovisual equipment before using it in a presentation. Nothing can unnerve you faster than an overhead projector with a blown bulb, an upside-down slide, the wrong video cassette in the machine, or any other equipment foul-up. A last-minute equipment check can prevent an embarrassing situation that can throw your entire meeting off schedule. Yes, checking the room and audiovisual equipment and making the attendees comfortable takes extra time and preparation, but neglecting to do so can lead to disaster. On the other hand, when you know everything is right for you and your audience, your confidence as a meeting leader will quickly grow.

Rule 6: Keep your meeting to less than an hour

It's ironic that while some shy people avoid one-to-one conversations, they can drone on for what seems for ever in a meeting. When it comes to time spent in meetings, less is more. In fact, some meetings might not even be necessary. Your supervisor might want you to take a meeting for one or more of the following reasons:

- To distribution information.
- To collect information.
- To collect ideas.
- To problem-solve in a group.
- To make a group decision.
- To offer recognition to staff.

If you cannot accomplish the goals of the meeting in an hour or less, revise your agenda and consider other ways to communicate with the staff.

Rule 7: Start on time and with a smile

Shy meeting leaders sometimes feel reluctant to get down to business before all the attendees are present – even if that means starting ten minutes late. However, nothing can be more frustrating to busy colleagues who get to a meeting on time than being forced to wait for latecomers. Starting meetings late punishes the punctual, rewards the tardy, wastes everyone's time, and wreaks havoc on your timetable and agenda. On the other hand, when you consistently start your meetings on time, most people will arrive promptly, and you'll stay on schedule. Moreover, people will respect your authority and ability to control the meeting. If a particular individual has a history of lateness, be assertive with them.

Don't forget to welcome everyone with a warm and friendly smile. After all, you have invited them to attend the meeting, so be a good host.

Rule 8: Control the pace of the meeting

Controlling the pace of the meeting is one of the leader's primary responsibilities. When you move through the agenda at a comfortable yet brisk pace, the people in the meeting will see you as confident and well organized. You do not have to be a dictator or a sourpuss to get the job done. Show your sense of humour and have a little fun too. A quip or little joke usually makes people feel more relaxed and keeps them tuned in to the meeting.

Rule 9: End on time and don't forget to say thank you

Many shy meeting leaders hesitate to bring certain open-ended discussions to an end, which can make the meeting run late. Make it your policy to end your meetings on time or earlier. If you have unfinished business, then plan it for another meeting or find another way to get it done. Take the last few minutes of the meeting to recap the main points covered, take any last questions, and thank everyone for their time and contributions.

Rule 10: Provide follow-up and feedback

Disorganized or inexperienced meeting leaders often forget promises they make to meeting attendees. To save yourself embarrassment, make a note to yourself about any follow-up actions you agreed to. Following up promptly with any information or action that you promised builds your credibility as a meeting leader. You can also increase participation in the next meeting when you offer a few private words of feedback and recognition to those who made extra contributions to the meeting. This is a particularly effective technique for encouraging further participation from shy attendees.

Handling difficult people in a meeting

For a shy person, leading a meeting can be nerve-racking, especially if you have a few difficult people in the group. If you let them, these troublesome individuals will try to undercut your credibility by wrestling away your control of the meeting. When that happens, you'll be left looking foolish, frustrated and diminished in the eyes of your peers and supervisors. It may not be easy, but when you prove to hard-to-handle people that you are confident and in control of the situation, they usually back off.

In many situations, you will need to interrupt difficult people. First say, 'Excuse me'. Then use the person's name. Always end your comment to the person with a polite 'Thanks' or 'I appreciate your co-operation'.

The following examples identify four typical groups of difficult people that you are likely to face in a meeting, and what you can do and say in response to their problem behaviour.

'Monopolizers' love the sound of their own voices

'Monopolizers' are constant talkers who interrupt, ramble endlessly, and say the same thing three different ways. You will probably need to interrupt them in order to stop them droning on.

How to deal with a Monopolizer

Wait for the Monopolizer to take a breath and then interrupt him or her. If you wait longer than a second you'll miss your best chance to cut off the Monopolizer. Use his or her name, paraphrase the main point, and ask someone else to talk.

Don't argue with these sometimes aggressive and intimidating people, but don't be shy about confronting them either. Monopolizers interrupt repeatedly to test your resolve and control. Remember, when you take a meeting, you call the shots.

'Distractors' are attention-seeking people

'Distractors' frequently bring up topics or ask questions outside the scope or purpose of the meeting. If you ask for sales figures, they want to know about insurance claims. When you discuss production schemes, they ask a question or begin a story about computer training. Distractors are usually poor listeners who have difficulty staying tuned in to one subject. They can ruin your meeting by wasting time and diffusing your focus.

How to deal with a Distractor

Respectfully and firmly interrupt the Distractor and restate the purpose of the meeting. Then address a specific question to the Distractor to help him or her focus on the main topic of discussion. If necessary, you can approach the Distractor after the meeting and address his or her issue on a one-to-one basis.

Remain determined not to answer the Distractor's questions or let him or her continue talking about a subject that falls outside the scope of the meeting.

'Sceptics' love pouring cold water on other people's ideas

'Sceptics' are those pessimistic pooh-poohers who see it as their duty to find fault in everything you or anyone else says or does. They undermine your credibility, and particularly discourage shy attendees from participating. These negative individuals can destroy a meeting in which the purpose is to generate ideas and solutions.

How to deal with a Sceptic

Don't let your shyness prevent you from stopping a Sceptic in his or her tracks. Before the meeting, have a firm but friendly talk with that person about your expectations. Explain how his or her often judgemental comments can inhibit the flow of ideas from others and that you want suggestions, not criticism. If the Sceptic's negative comments persist during the meeting, respectfully remind him or her that you are seeking possible solutions – not criticism. Then throw the ball into the Sceptic's court by asking for a contribution.

Don't lose your cool. Tempting as it may be, do not scold, criticize or put Sceptics down in front of the group, because they can be vindictive and may try to undermine your authority. A private word with the Sceptic during the break may get better results.

'Snipers' make snide remarks during the meeting

Sometimes 'Snipers' are witty and funny, but the humour is usually at your expense. Their goal is to challenge your authority and move the attention away from you and on to them.

How to deal with a Sniper

Do not be shy about confronting these sneaky people, because if you want to retain control of the meeting, you will need to make them stop their undermining behaviour. Call attention to Snipers by asking them to share their comments with everyone else in the meeting. Most often, Snipers will decline the invitation out of embarrassment. However, if they do share a good-natured joke, then give them a laugh and get back to the agenda. Again, a quiet word with the Sniper before the meeting or during a short break can often eliminate his or her disruptive behaviour.

Be strong and keep your sense of humour, but do not let them off the hook. Snipers can make some positive contributions and bring valid points into the open if you encourage them with a firm request and a smile. Keep in mind, though, that Snipers, like Sceptics, do not respond well to public criticism or chiding and can become vindictive when they get angry.

Well-planned meetings are productive and fun

When you set your objectives, plan your agenda and tell the attendees how they can contribute, your meetings will be enjoyable and productive. By interjecting a little humour into your meetings, you will encourage attendance and participation. Plus, for a shy person like you, leading a meeting will be more enjoyable and rewarding.

DOS AND DON'TS FOR PRODUCTIVE MEETINGS

Do:

✓ Be informal and upbeat.
✓ Come with goodies to eat.
✓ Display finished products.
✓ Focus on achievements.
✓ Introduce and welcome new staff.
✓ Offer personal congratulations.
✓ Provide a fun theme when possible.
✓ Recognize and thank the attendees.
✓ Tell clean jokes or insightful stories.

Don't:

✗ Argue over differences in public.
✗ Ask people to speak without warning.
✗ Be late to your own meeting.
✗ Chastise an attendee in front of other colleagues.
✗ Deal with individual problems.
✗ Abide by your attendees' schedules and not yours.
✗ Make others wait for latecomers.
✗ Take outside phone calls.
✗ Waste time on non-agenda items.

12

Giving an informative speech

Every speaker's greatest fear

Author Thomas Heggen was scheduled to speak at a luncheon about his new book, *Mister Roberts*. As Mr Heggen stood before the audience, he froze and was unable to utter a single word. Seeing his extreme distress and wanting to help, a fellow guest leaned over and said, 'Perhaps you can tell us how you came to write your book.' Mr Heggen suddenly came alive and the words began to flow. 'Well, [expletive deleted],' he said, 'it was just that I was on this boat and . . .'

If you break out in a cold sweat at the thought of giving a speech, you are in good company. Even professional speakers with years of experience often feel anxious during the first few moments of their presentations, but they conquer their nervousness by following the two basic principles of public speaking – preparation and practice. Whether you are a seasoned speaker or shy neophyte, carefully structuring the content of what you plan to say and honing your platform skills will result in a confident and successful presentation.

Organizing your speech

If you are highly skilled or informed, someone may call upon you to give a speech. Perhaps a chairperson has asked you to speak at a charity fund-raising dinner, a professional meeting or a community organization, or you've been asked on behalf of your company to address a public forum. Whether you speak before a small or large group, structuring your informative speech with a beginning, middle and end helps create an inspiring and memorable presentation. Speakers usually organize informative speeches into three parts – the opening, main body and conclusion. It may surprise you, but most professional speakers develop the main body of their speech first and then write their opening and conclusion afterwards.

Part 1: Outline the main body of your informative speech
What are you going to talk about? When choosing a topic, consider

this advice from professional speakers: speak about what you know and always prepare your presentation. An informative speech can be about any number of topics, depending on your areas of expertise and your audience.

Presentation tip: To overcome 'presentation anxiety', remember that you were asked to give a speech because others consider you an 'expert' in the field, or you are someone who can share a meaningful experience with an audience. In most cases, your audience wants to hear what you have to say. You are in a powerful position of influence because you have an opportunity to change people's lives for the better.

Organize the body of your speech around a purpose and central idea

Before you begin preparing your speech, ask yourself a few questions. Why is your topic important to the audience? How are they going to benefit from what you have to tell them? What is the primary message that you want to convey? To answer these questions, learn as much as possible about your audience's goals and challenges. Once you understand the needs of your audience, you can organize the central idea.

Presentation tip: If you make a major mistake or 'freeze', collect your thoughts and start again. If you make a minor mistake, then just continue talking. No one will know you bungled it except you.

Now you have a topic for your speech, but that's just the first step. Next, you need to organize your ideas. To help you visualize the structure of an informative speech, imagine a triangle. Within the body of your speech, the purpose and central idea are at the top. Next come the main points, followed by examples, facts, quotations and anecdotes. Write your speech's purpose, main points and supporting facts on a pad of paper. Now you have an outline to work with.

Presentation tip: The main points are the linchpins of your speech. If you lose your place while speaking, go back to the main point and then pick up where you left off. Highlighting the main points keeps you on track and helps your audience understand the purpose and ideas in your speech.

Make your speech come alive with colourful examples

Now that you have a simple outline of your informative speech, make your topic come alive by including colourful examples, facts, quotations and anecdotes. Think of a catchy title for your speech that encompasses its central idea and purpose. Continually connect the central idea of your speech to the needs and goals of the audience. Remember that each person listening wants to know 'What's in it for me?'

If you are not careful, you might overwhelm your audience with too many facts or too much technical language. Use everyday words that the audience members can visualize and understand – not jargon – unless they have a working knowledge of the subject. Be sure to illustrate your main points with examples and stories that your listeners can identify with. Always avoid abstract theories or anecdotes with twisted plots. Whether you plan to write and memorize your speech or speak off-the-cuff, lively supporting details add sparkle to your presentation.

Part 2: Begin your speech with a 'hook'

For a shy person, the opening moments of a speech can be a paralysing experience. Why do you think most professional speakers write and memorize the openings of their speeches? They know that they have only a minute or two to 'hook' their audience's interest and to establish cedibility as a speaker. In addition, a good introduction quickly gets the audience on the speaker's side. If, after a few minutes, people in the audience say to themselves 'So what?', the speaker is in big trouble. That is why you need to use a strong opening statement to catch your audience's attention. The following examples are just a few of the many ways you can begin your speech.

Presentation tip: Overcome the fear that you will forget what to say by writing the main points of your outline on individual note cards. Then turn them over one at a time as you give your talk 'off-the-cuff'. Your outline allows you to be carefully organized and yet still sound spontaneous.

Pose an evocative question

One easy way for a shy person to quickly involve the audience is to ask a thought-provoking question. This effective opening captures an audience's attention because each member will answer it automatically.

Presentation tip: Overcome nervousness by taking a few seconds to prepare yourself before you begin talking. Plant your feet, slightly bending your knees, and smile at your audience. Now you are ready to speak.

Quote a relevant source

You can quote a celebrity, industry expert, humorist, proverb or slogan to grab your audience's attention. Be sure to choose words that will be meaningful to the audience and quote them accurately.

Presentation tip: Know your quote by heart so you can look directly at the audience when you open your presentation.

Share a personal experience

While a shy person may feel a little uncomfortable sharing a personal experience, most audiences love to hear 'triumph against all odds' stories. If you have a good one, use it, but keep it concise, genuine and connected to your speech's central point.

Presentation tip: When telling a dramatic story, modulate your voice so that you're speaking softly and in a controlled manner. Do not overplay the emotional aspect of the story for the sake of effect. Just tell the story as if you were relating the events to a group of close friends.

Cite a dramatic fact or trend

Opening your speech with a dramatic fact is another easy way for you to make a strong impact on your audience. However, be sure to follow up any unsettling information with ways that the audience can help change the situation.

Presentation tip: Use props to emphasize key points and draw attention to yourself. Make sure the props are large enough for people at the back to see.

Part 3: Write and memorize the conclusion of your speech

If you are a shy or inexperienced speaker, you might be so anxious to stop speaking that you overlook a critical part of your presentation – the conclusion. On the other hand, many professional speakers write the concluding words of their speech because they know that the last few words and thoughts the audience hears are usually the ones they remember most. To effectively conclude your speech, be sure to:

- Recap the central idea and main points.
- End on a positive note – with a bang!

Recap the central idea and main points

Even the best listeners in your audience need to hear your central idea and a few main points summarized at the end of your speech. This not only signals that the end is near, but a summary reinforces your message.

End your speech on a positive note – with a bang!

The end of a successful speech puts a smile on people's faces and motivates them to take action. Be sure to *complete any unfinished story* that you stopped earlier. You can also end with a dramatic statement or quotation that sums up everything you have said. Be sure to conclude on a positive note and, when it applies, ask for a commitment.

Presentation tip: Always smile at the audience when you finish your speech. Don't just end with the words 'Thank you' or 'That's it' and walk away. A friendly wave of your hand is a good way to say 'thank you' and 'goodbye' to your audience.

Do you want to memorize, read or speak off-the-cuff?

Some speakers prefer to memorize their speeches, while others like to read them. Still others like to talk off-the-cuff from a prepared outline. The best speakers employ techniques from all three methods. They may memorize their opening and closing statements, spontaneously follow a carefully prepared outline for the rest, and stop and read a paragraph or two from a business journal at some point. No matter which style you choose, practice plays a vital role in the successful presentation of your speech.

Practice points for poised presentations

Nothing builds platform skills and confidence like practice. No matter how short a speech or how well you know the subject matter, nothing excuses you from taking the time to practise your presentation. You simply will not do your best if you neglect to practise your speech out loud and often. As you practise, use these simple yet effective tips to help you present your speech with poise and confidence:

- Start practising immediately and continue right up to the time of your presentation.
- Visualize a warm and smiling audience.
- Practise your opening sentence – word for word – at least five times in a row.
- Practise your presentation aloud at least five times before you present it in public.
- Repeat the words slowly so you can clearly hear all the syllables.
- Open and close your mouth and puff up your cheeks to relax your jaws and mouth.
- Practise in front of a mirror, a tape recorder, a camcorder or a supportive audience.
- Use hand gestures to emphasize your main points.
- Vary the volume, tone and pace of your voice to express feelings and energy.
- Memorize and practise the sequence of your main ideas.
- Memorize and practise the transitions from main idea to main idea.
- Keep to your allotted time to speak.

Public speaking skills will boost your confidence

It can be more than a little nerve-racking for a shy person to make a speech, yet the pay-offs can be tremendous for the audience – and for your self-confidence. When you organize your main ideas and support them with plenty of interesting facts, examples and stories, you will keep your listeners hanging on to your every word. By carefully crafting your opening and closing statements, you will start your speech in a way that will instantly capture your audience's attention and end it with a bang that will leave them applauding. Then the only thing left for you to do will be to smile, bow, and look forward to your next speaking engagement!

WHAT NOT TO SAY WHEN SPEAKING OFF-THE-CUFF

Making an off-the-cuff presentation is especially challenging for the shy person. The best impromptu speeches are short and relevant. With only a few minutes to prepare, you'll probably only have time to write down your central idea. Support it with three main points, plus a few examples. Here are ten common mistakes to avoid in an impromptu talk:

- Apologizing or making excuses for what you are about to say.
- Scolding the person who asked you to say a few words.
- Stalling for longer than 45 seconds.
- Beginning with a story unless you have had success with it in a similar situation.
- Telling a long story.
- Providing too many facts, examples or detailed explanations.
- Citing questionable or controversial sources.
- Detracting from your main points with obscure examples.
- Revealing proprietary information.
- Not knowing when to stop talking.

13

'Soft-selling' your way to confidence

Opportunity knocks for the shy person

Help! Your boss has just come into your office and complimented you on the great job you have done behind the scenes as a children's textbook editor. That's the good news – all your hard work has been recognized. The bad news is that she wants you to 'sell' the reading scheme to several school administrators at an important meeting. After you scrape yourself up off the floor, you explain that you are 'very shy' and that you don't know the first thing about selling. 'Don't worry,' she chuckles. 'Just give them a bit of the "soft-sell".'

As a shy person you may find the idea of 'selling' unappealing because it conjures up visions of the shifty sales rep or a high-pressure car salesman. In reality, most professional salespeople use 'soft-selling' techniques to communicate their message and clinch the sale. Soft-selling uses gentle persuasion instead of aggressive, high-pressure tactics to convince someone to buy your product or service. Many professionals who do not consider themselves 'salespeople' use soft-selling skills. For example, a financial adviser or pensions salesperson soft-sells financial security by persuading people to pay into a private pension plan. For shy people who do not want to appear aggressive, soft-selling techniques are an especially effective way to deliver a low-pressure sales presentation. You can master the art of soft-selling by following these four steps:

THE FOUR STEPS OF SOFT-SELLING

Step 1: Establish credibility and trust with a rapport-building statement.

Step 2: Ask questions and listen to uncover a client's needs.

Step 3: Outline the benefits and advantages of what you are selling.

Step 4: Clinch the deal by actually asking for the order.

Step 1: Establish credibility and trust with a rapport-building statement

In Chapter 4 you learned how to establish credibility and trust in the first few seconds of a conversation. You can use some of these very same skills when you do a sales presentation. One fast and effective way to establish rapport is to begin your presentation with a statement that shows that you understand the client's needs.

Step 2: Ask questions and listen to uncover a client's needs

Most skilled salespersons do not go into meetings and spread out their wares on the table like a flea market trader. They know that first they must ask questions to uncover the client's needs before explaining the benefits and features of a product or service. Once you know your client's needs, you can tailor your soft-sell message accordingly.

Use the '80/20' rule of listening and talking

Being shy, you are probably a good listener. At a sales meeting, you will need to put that all-important communication skill to work. Soft-selling requires that you listen 80 per cent of the time and talk only 20 per cent of the time – which is probably just fine with you! Successful salespeople ask the right questions at the proper time and then listen carefully to their client's answers.

Use the 80/20 rule of listening and talking so that your client does most of the talking. Remember that even if you know your client's needs, let him or her express them.

Step 3: Outline the benefits and advantages of what you are selling

People skilled at soft-selling know that buyers make a decision by connecting the perceived benefits of a product or service with its specific features.

Present the product or service you wish to soft-sell in terms of how your client will benefit from its features. If you omit the benefits from a sales presentation, this question remains in the client's mind: 'OK, all those gizmos are fine and dandy, but how is this software program (equipment, training, etc.) going to help me solve my problem?'

Be specific when you link features to benefits. Begin your 'benefits statement' with something like this: 'The benefits of using this product or service are . . .' Then include a few value-enhancing words and phrases such as:

- Cost-cutting performance.
- Decreases waste.
- Dependable parts and service.
- Economical to operate.
- Energy efficient.
- Environmentally safe.
- Extra features and options.
- Greater client satisfaction.
- High quality.
- Increased profits.
- Simplifies procedures.
- State-of-the-art.
- Unsurpassed performance.

- Healthier workforce.
- Fewer staff turnovers.
- Increased employee motivation.
- Lasting value.
- Maximizes productivity.
- Recyclable.
- Reduces downtime.
- Reliable.
- Safe to handle.
- Saves time and money.
- Faster turnarounds.
- Happier customers.
- Greater employee commitment.

Note: Choose only three or four of the most important benefits that address your client's needs, otherwise your soft-sell presentation turns into a benefits speech that borders on a 'hard-sell'.

Step 4: Clinch the deal by actually asking for the order

In Chapter 1 you learned how positive self-talk can build up your confidence. At the end of your sales presentation, you can use self-talk to help you confidently ask the client to buy your product or service. If your doubting inner voice says 'She's not convinced' or 'I know he'll say no if I ask', your confidence will plummet, along with your chances of getting the sale. Don't allow negative self-talk to jeopardize your soft-sell presentation. Instead, say to yourself,

'My product or service is an effective solution for this client's problem.'

Asking for a decision to buy is sometimes called 'closing the sale'. As a shy person, you may find that closing a sale is very daunting. As a result, you hesitate to ask for the order because you do not want to appear to be pushy and aggressive, or to hear the word 'No'. So replace any negative self-talk with positive messages and get ready to try a 'test' closing.

Now is the time for a 'test' closing

See if your client is receptive to your soft-sell by trying a test closing. Make sure you have linked the features and benefits of your product or service to your client's needs. Now test to see if the client is ready to make a commitment by saying something like: 'Do you feel comfortable with the outline (proposal, workshop, textbooks, etc.) I've suggested?'

Take the risk and ask for the sale

If you get a positive response to a test closing, take the presentation to the next step and ask for the sale. It takes some courage, but what a confidence-booster when the person says 'Yes'! The following is an example of just one way of many of asking for the sale: 'When would you like to begin?'

Dealing with objections

Do not be surprised if your client hesitates when you try a test closing or ask for the sale. Pausing is natural for people as they consider making any financial commitment. Give them time to think and *do not pressure them* to decide. As you learned earlier in Chapters 4 and 12, preparation leads to effective presentations. It also leads to confident closings in which you are ready with the right answers. If your client has objections, repeat the key (not negative) words in the objection and then address them. Be sure to emphasize the benefits of your product or service to the client.

Save small talk for the end of the meeting

While some clients avoid small talk entirely, others enjoy brief and informal chats with the people they do business with. A minute or two of friendly conversation after you have discussed business usually helps to build the professional and personal relationship, especially after the first meeting.

Remember that for busy people, spending more than a few minutes making small talk at the end of a business meeting might be considered unprofessional. However, if you discover a common interest with a client, you might suggest meeting for an informal lunch (drink, game of golf, tennis, etc.) to continue the conversation and to get to know each other better.

Soft-selling is a great confidence-builder

You will be pleasantly surprised to find that a reserved person like you can become more outgoing when you soft-sell a valued product or service. By establishing rapport and using the four-step soft-selling process, you'll learn a valuable new set of communication skills that will enhance your career opportunities. Even more important, you'll discover that your confidence and self-esteem will grow too, because what you are really soft-selling is you!

14

Negotiating successful agreements

You are always negotiating

A colleague wants to swap her day off with yours so that she can attend her old-school reunion. Your manager wants you to handle customers' complaints along with your other responsibilities. You want to work part time from home so that you can spend more time with your children. An important client presses you to cut the price of an order because of her department's budget shortfall. Another day, another negotiation, and if you are shy but not careful, you could end up with a raw deal. Your goal in these situations is to negotiate satisfactory agreements for both you and your colleagues, bosses, clients and family. When that happens, you have negotiated a 'win-win' agreement.

Preparing for negotiations increases your confidence

Because shy people often avoid confrontations or fear offending others, they can be in danger of getting less than they want. How can you avoid feeling uncomfortable when you need to negotiate an agreement? What can you do to stop saying the wrong thing, settling for less than you deserve, or getting talked into an unprofitable agreement? How can you negotiate an agreement whereby both you and the other party are pleased with the outcome?

As a shy person entering a negotiation with a highly aggressive or skilled opponent, you might feel like David fighting Goliath. However, in Chapter 2 you learned how to identify many of your abilities and achievements to boost your self-confidence. You can use the same strategy to project a confident image and firm stance as you enter the negotiating arena. You can also decrease your anxiety and increase your chances of a successful negotiation by using the following five negotiating strategies.

Five strategies that lead to 'win-win' agreements

The key to completing a successful negotiation rests on these five primary factors:

1 Negotiate both parties' main interests – not their fixed positions.
2 Ask questions to explore mutually beneficial options.
3 Develop an alternative, or 'walk-away', plan to an unsatisfactory offer.
4 Cite examples that show the agreement is fair.
5 Develop an implementation plan.

Strategy 1: Negotiate both parties' main interests – not their fixed positions

Shy or unskilled negotiators often bargain from inflexible, or 'fixed', positions instead of discussing their main interests. Here is one example of bargaining from a fixed position:

Bob, the printer: *'I need a rise of £30 a week or I may have to leave.'*

Tina, the owner of a print shop: *'I can only afford an extra £10 a week. That's it!'*

In this negotiation Bob demands a higher rise than Tina is willing to pay. Bob and Tina have framed their negotiation around the fixed position of money, leaving only four possible outcomes, none of which completely satisfies either party's main interests.

Possible outcome no. 1: Tina wins and Bob loses

Bob feels cheated, so he becomes less productive and considers finding a job at another print shop. While Tina wins in the short term, Bob's productivity drops. As a result, Bob gets a job with her main rival. This leaves Tina with the time-consuming and expensive task of finding a suitable replacement.

Possible outcome no. 2: Bob wins and Tina loses

Tina feels that Bob pressurized her into an unprofitable agreement. She fears that without him she cannot fill several large forthcoming orders. In addition, the money that she budgeted to upgrade outdated printing equipment must now go on Bob's increased salary. Tina sees Bob as an expense she cannot afford and decides to eventually replace him with a cheaper employee.

Possible outcome no. 3: No agreement

Bob and Tina dig in their heels and refuse to move from their fixed positions. Their negotiations end in stalemate. Soon Bob is looking for a new job and Tina is looking for a new employee. This lose-lose agreement leaves both Bob and Tina in a worse position than they were before they started their negotiations.

Possible outcome no. 4: Tina and Bob compromise

After threats and tense words, Bob and Tina 'split the difference' on the money issue and agree on an increase in Bob's salary. Though this agreement is based on a compromise, both Tina and Bob feel that they got less than they wanted and, as a result, their working relationship suffers. Bob wants to leave when he can find a job that pays more money and Tina wants to employ someone who is more cost-effective. Both Bob and Tina remain stuck in their new fixed positions until their next negotiation, when they will repeat the whole frustrating process.

Revealing mutual interests leads to win-win agreements

Negotiating from fixed positions like Tina and Bob did was definitely not a winning strategy for either of them. But Tina and Bob had another negotiating alternative. They could have created a win-win agreement if they looked beyond their fixed positions and negotiated around their mutual interests. Tina and Bob must reveal to each other why they want what they want, and understand the purpose behind their respective positions. When each person steps into the other's shoes, the chances for achieving a win-win agreement increase. Let's compare Bob's and Tina's main interests and concerns.

Bob's interests and concerns

- ✓ Pay off credit card debt.
- ✓ Move to a larger flat.
- ✓ Buy a wedding ring for fiancée.
- ✓ Repair fishing boat.
- ✓ Buy electric saw for his side business.
- ✓ Needs higher-paying job.
- ✓ Wants to learn new job skills.
- ✓ Wants promotion opportunities.
- ✓ Wants a position with more prestige.
- ✓ Does not want to look for a new job.

Tina's interests and concerns

- ✓ Run a profitable business.
- ✓ Maintain lowest overheads possible.
- ✓ Upgrade printing equipment.
- ✓ Expand product sales.
- ✓ Spend more time with family.
- ✓ Not lose customers to competitors.
- ✓ Find responsible shop manager.
- ✓ Keep hard-working employees.
- ✓ Avoid cost of hiring a new employee.
- ✓ Add a room for new equipment.

Negotiate from areas of mutual interest

Once Tina and Bob bring their interests and concerns to the negotiating table, they can see where their interests coincide. For example, perhaps Tina will consider training Bob as the shop manager. This would fulfil Tina's desire to spend more time with her family, and it would also fulfil Bob's desire for a job with more opportunity for promotion, status and income. When they work together to explore additional options, they will find that the potential for a win-win agreement increases even more.

Clarify your goals

Before you start negotiating for anything, write the answers to these questions on a sheet of paper to help clarify your main interests.

Encouraging the other party to do the same can make your negotiations less stressful and more productive:

'What do I really want and why?'

'What are my needs?'

'What concerns me?'

'What do I want to accomplish in the short term and in the long term?'

'Who else has a stake in these negotiations?'

Pitfalls

Avoid these common mistakes when defining your interests:

✗ Assuming your interests and those of your counterpart conflict.
✗ Not clearly identifying your main interests to the other party.
✗ Not asking your counterpart to identify his or her main interests.
✗ Assuming your concerns are the same as your counterpart's.
✗ Assuming you know the interests and concerns of your counterpart without asking.
✗ Not listening for implied interests that your counterpart fails to make clear.

Strategy 2: Ask questions to explore mutually beneficial options

As a shy person, you can increase your confidence and bargaining position by talking about mutually beneficial options. When you and your counterpart identify areas of common concern, then you can find several possible satisfactory solutions. Once Tina and Bob identify and discuss their interests, they can explore options by answering a series of questions.

'Where do our interests and concerns overlap?'

Mutual interests: Bob wants a stable job and Tina wants reliable workers. Bob wants a job with future opportunities and Tina wants to hire a shop manager.

Option: Tina agrees to promote Bob to manager and increase his salary if he is willing to work more hours.

'What can we do for each other that requires little investment of our respective time and money?'

Mutual interests: Expand sales and job opportunities to make more money.

Option: Bob sold printing services and trained new employees in his last job. If Tina promotes him to shop manager, he can do the same for her. Tina can teach Bob how to use the store computer to track orders and let him use the company car to make sales visits.

'How can we use our different skills and resources to fulfil our interests?'

Mutual interests: Both Tina and Bob want flexible working hours.

Option: Tina prefers to begin work before 7.30 a.m. and leave by 4.00 p.m. so that she can be home for dinner with her family. Bob is willing to work later and close the shop at 6.00 p.m. in return for coming at about 9.30 a.m.

'What skills and resources do we share that can help us achieve our respective goals?'

Mutual interests: Tina and Bob know different aspects of the printing business. To increase their productivity and income, each needs to learn more about what the other knows.

Option: Tina and Bob can team up on certain sales calls. As they share their individual expertise in answering business and technical questions, they can each add to the business's productivity.

'What creative options can we explore that will expand the total benefits to both of us?'

Mutual interests: Bob has a side business as a carpenter and Tina wants to build additional space for a new bookbinding machine.

Option: Tina could employ Bob to build an extension to the print shop so it could hold a bookbinding machine. By expanding into the bookbinding market, Bob and Tina increase the opportunities to fulfil their interests.

Strategy 3: Develop an alternative, or 'walk-away', plan to an unsatisfactory offer

A shy person may feel like 'giving in' and accepting a bad deal if the negotiations seem to be going downhill – and, of course, that is exactly what the other side is betting on. Have you thought about what your options are in the event that you do not negotiate an acceptable agreement with your counterpart? If you identify a course of action in which you will 'walk away' from the negotiations, it helps to protect you from entering into an agreement you will later regret. It also builds confidence because it clearly identifies the situation in which your option *not* to negotiate is the best course of action to follow. For example, if Bob had a firm job offer from another printer, he could exercise this option as a 'walk-away' plan. Bob's new job offer may not be ideal, but if it is better than an unsatisfactory pay increase from Tina, then it may be considered an acceptable 'walk-away' plan.

Pitfalls
Avoid these common mistakes when exploring a 'walk-away' plan:

✗ Threatening to leave the negotiation without a clearly defined 'walk-away' plan.
✗ Developing an unrealistic 'walk-away' plan.
✗ Ending negotiations before discussing all the issues.

Strategy 4: Cite examples that show the agreement is fair

Shy people are typically more concerned about being fair and maintaining a good relationship than are their more aggressive counterparts, who want everything they can get out of a negotiation.

How do you know if an agreement that you or your counterpart proposes is fair? Win-win agreements require that no one feel cheated after entering into an agreement. To build your confidence about the fairness of an agreement, find out what others have negotiated under similar circumstances. Make a few phone calls to friends, colleagues or other informed sources to ask for advice from someone with experience. Be sure to look for precedents that support the positions of both parties.

For example, perhaps a travel agent protests that the price you quoted her for a block of hotel rooms is too expensive for her conference clients. Being shy and not wanting to offend a client, you might cave in and drop your price. However, you can remain firm and yet still calm her fear of entering into a poor agreement by confidently referring to industry standards, citing specific examples, and recalling past agreements with the same or similar clients.

Use these additional sources to support your negotiations:

- Annual reports.
- Association guidelines.
- Competitive shopping.
- Independent tests and surveys.
- Industry publications.
- Media reviews.

- Newspaper articles.
- People in similar jobs.
- Previous agreements.
- Price guides.
- Professional regulations.
- Recent comparable sales.

Help your counterpart to sell your agreement to other interested parties

Shy people aren't the only ones who may be uncomfortable negotiating agreements. In today's world of team decision-making, your counterpart is probably not the only person who has to agree to the terms of your proposal. Typically, your counterpart may need to clear your agreement with his or her superiors, board of directors, lawyers or others who have a stake in the negotiations. By including similar contracts or written examples to show your requests are fair, you can help your counterpart justify the agreement to the other parties involved.

Pitfalls

Avoid these common mistakes when citing examples to show a fair agreement.

94

Do not:

✗ Refer to outdated information or regulations.
✗ Offer precedents from distinctly different industries.
✗ Reveal privileged or confidential information.
✗ Assume that your counterpart shares your standards of fairness.

Strategy 5: Develop an implementation plan

'Promises may make friends, but 'tis performances that keep them.' (old proverb)

If you are a bit shy, you may feel uncomfortable asking your counterpart to 'sign on the dotted line'. The truth is, however, a negotiated agreement is only as good as its commitment to action. Therefore, to make sure that your win-win agreement becomes a reality, also negotiate an implementation plan that includes a timetable and clear description of what constitutes a completed agreement.

Following up on commitments completes win-win agreements

Here is where a shy person can really show that he or she is confident and competent. After you agree to certain commitments, negotiate how to execute the agreement. During this part of your negotiations get answers to questions such as:

'How are we going to carry out our agreement?'

'Who is responsible for carrying out the various aspects of the agreement?'

'What obstacles may prevent our agreement from being completed?'

'How are we going to deal with unforeseen obstacles?'

'Is our agreement contingent on the fulfilling of an agreement with others?'

'When can we expect to complete the agreement?'

'What constitutes a completed agreement?'

'What happens if either party fails to fulfil its part of the agreement?'

Get your business agreements in writing

Congratulations! You might be shy, but you and your counterpart have negotiated an excellent deal. However, you still need to complete one more vital component before you can crack open the bottle of bubbly, clink glasses, and say, 'We've got a deal!' **Ask to get the agreement in writing**. Most businesses use signed contracts or letters of agreement to complete their agreements, and for good reason. As time passes, people often forget what terms and responsibilities they agreed to. Furthermore, signed agreements set precedents for future negotiations. And finally, if differences of opinion arise between parties, a signed agreement can help clarify misunderstandings and resolve disputes. In the example with Bob and Tina, a simple letter stating Bob's new job description and salary may be enough to clarify their agreement and to avoid any misunderstandings later.

Pitfalls

Avoid these common mistakes when following up on commitments:

✗ Relying on verbal agreements or your memory.
✗ Not keeping to the spirit of the agreement.
✗ Assuming agreements with friends or family do not need to be in writing.
✗ Not reading the agreements that you have signed.
✗ Not confronting major infractions of your agreement.

Remain firm yet flexible when you negotiate

There may be situations when emotions escalate and a conflict of interest arises between you and your counterpart. Do you remember in Chapter 7 that you learned not to overreact or argue if you are verbally attacked, but instead to listen for and seek common ground?

The trick during your negotiations is to remain firm yet flexible. If the other person tries to intimidate or pressure you into an agreement that is not in your best interests, then call for a short break. To remain cool and calm, visualize how you want the negotiations to conclude. While you may want to let your counterpart blow off some steam, don't wait too long to confront him or her. You can calmly say, 'As far as I am concerned, yelling, intimidation and pressure tactics are not part of this negotiation.' Flexibility in negotiations is vital, but not when it comes to your self-respect. In most cases, if you calmly let your counterpart know you will not tolerate intimidation or pressure tactics, he or she will back off and both of you can get back to reaching an agreement.

Negotiate with confidence and everyone wins

Being shy doesn't mean that you can't get what you want. Once you have your information, negotiating strategies and 'walk-away' plan in place, you are ready to negotiate with employers, colleagues, clients or anyone else. When you know your own main interests as well as those of your counterpart, and search for mutually beneficial options, you'll be on your way to negotiating win-win agreements.

TEN TIPS FOR BETTER NEGOTIATIONS

1 Go into every negotiation with the strongest 'walk-away' option possible.
2 Put yourself in the other person's shoes to understand his or her interests.
3 Focus on mutual interests, not fixed positions.
4 If you reach an impasse, take a break and come back with new options.
5 Anticipate your counterpart's objections to an agreement and formulate other options beforehand.
6 Deal with the main issues, not the personality of the negotiator.
7 If you are at an impasse, restate your position and interests in a different way.
8 Look for ways that you and your counterpart can combine skills and resources to create better options than the ones you are presently negotiating for.
9 Refer to other agreements to avoid getting roped into an unsatisfactory agreement.
10 Stall high-pressure negotiators by saying, 'I'll think about it and call you later.'

15

Dealing with difficult clients

Communicating with aggressive, passive and passive-aggressive clients

It is Monday morning and you have meetings scheduled with three of your most difficult clients. As a shy person, you always feel a little nervous meeting clients, but these three demanding individuals take it on to an entirely different level. One yells and screams like a sergeant major. The second says almost nothing, so you have no idea what she thinks. And the third always insists on giving you unsolicited advice on how to run your business. Then they blame you when things go wrong! After a day with these clients, you are usually ready to resign and change professions.

If you are shy, you may be particularly susceptible to difficult people and may avoid confronting them whenever possible. You may dream of telling them to 'take a running jump', but if you are like most people in business, you do not have the luxury of losing any clients – even the ones who sometimes drive you crazy! If left to their own devices, these difficult clients can waste your time and cost you money. However, by learning how to communicate with difficult clients, you can minimize their negative impact on you and your business.

There are many kinds of difficult clients, but most can be categorized as having aggressive, passive or passive-aggressive behaviour. If you focus on your clients' difficult behaviour – not their personalities – you can adopt effective communication strategies for dealing with them.

'Intimidators' and 'Pinballs' are aggressive clients

Aggressive clients will try to intimidate you so that they can have their way. These are high-energy individuals who take many risks and attempt to 'win through intimidation'. They care little about the needs and feelings of others, especially shy people like you! The two main types of aggressive clients are 'Intimidators' and 'Pinballs'.

99

Intimidators try to dominate others

Intimidators are aggressive cients who speak loudly, often swear, and may even use threatening physical gestures to get what they want. They storm into meetings, make sweeping accusations, and bark orders like sergeant majors. Intimidators have little time for polite conversation, but are always ready for an argument. These aggressive communicators speak impulsively, interrupt frequently, are poor listeners, and have a low tolerance for details. Their attitude is 'I don't care how you get it done – just do it!'

Intimidators leave you feeling coerced, emotionally battered, fearful and unappreciated. Their antagonistic communication style is particularly hard for shy people; these verbal bullies foster an uncomfortable or even hostile atmosphere that leads to mistakes, dissatisfaction and frequent staff turnover.

Stand up to Intimidators without arguing

While 'the customer is always right' is a good rule to apply when dealing with Intimidators, if you let them browbeat you, they can make you feel like an ill-treated dog. Since Intimidators love to fight, make sure you don't dig in your heels and argue with them. Instead, stand tall and listen carefully for issues that you can address. You can curb their dominating personality if you calmly define for them some respectful 'ground rules' for when they talk to you. Usually, Intimidators will back off when you stand up for yourself. If an Intimidator attacks you with a verbal barrage, let him or her blow off some steam and then follow these five assertive steps.

Step 1: Establish communication ground rules with the Intimidator

Intimidating clients know from experience that if they pressurize a shy person, he or she will probably cave in. You can respectfully establish the communication ground rules by using the Intimidator's name and saying something like the following:

> *'Excuse me, Mr . . . I would like to help you. The problem is that I can't understand you when you scream into the telephone. Would you please calmly explain the problem and what you would like me to do about it?'*

Step 2: Actively listen and paraphrase the Intimidator's comments

When an Intimidator challenges you, look him or her square in the eye and with a controlled voice say something like:

> '*I can see why you are upset about* . . . [be specific]. *That would bother me too.*'

Step 3: Disagree without debating

Intimidators often make unfair or inaccurate accusations just to incite an argument or intimidate shy people. When this happens, avoid the confrontation by simply disagreeing. For example, you can say:

> '*I see the situation in a rather different way.*'

If the Intimidator keeps up the verbal barrage, keep looking him or her in the eye but say nothing. Silence can be a powerful tool in dealing with an Intimidator. Stay calm and stand your ground even though you might feel like running out of the room. Remember that these aggressive people try to manipulate shy people with rudeness and intimidation. If you react with an angry outburst or defensive comment, they will see it as a challenge and escalate the situation into an argument, which they will probably win. If, on the other hand, you do not respond to their insults, the Intimidators usually run out of steam. When the Intimidator does pause for breath, calmly repeat in a controlled voice that you want to address his or her concerns if he or she can just calm down.

Step 4: Summarize main points for the Intimidator

In general, Intimidators are poor listeners, so you may need to repeat the main point several times. In a calm and clear voice, say something like:

> *Ms* . . . *These are the four issues as I understand them.*'

Step 5: Seek a negotiated compromise with the Intimidator

Intimidators usually ask for more than they really want. In Chapter 14 you learned to identify mutual interests, and this skill can help you deal with Intimidators too. Without giving in to all their demands, let them 'win' by agreeing to some, but not all, of their demands. This negotiating technique works only if you limit how much you are willing to compromise – otherwise, the Intimidator will see your compromise as the first of many, and will just keep pushing you for more concessions.

Do not be surprised if the Intimidator gets worked up again as your conversation progresses. If this happens, respectfully remind him or her that you are here to solve the problem, but only if the two of you can discuss it calmly.

Pinballs are aggressive clients who do not focus their activity

Pinballs are high-powered, aggressive clients who bounce around with so many ideas and so much energy that they are hard to control. Their minds and mouths ricochet from one 'great concept' to another, but they rarely develop their ideas to a logical conclusion. While they do not usually win through intimidation, Pinballs use their aggressive style and unbridled energy to overwhelm shy people who might be standing in their way.

Since Pinballs make impulsive decisions and then later change their minds, they waste your time and resources by sending you on wildgoose chases. Consequently, completing any project on time is difficult when your client is a Pinball.

Help Pinballs to focus on one task at a time

Pinballs equate their increased activity with a high level of achievement. However, in reality, they are often just 'spinning their wheels' and wasting time. An effective communication strategy for dealing with Pinballs is to slow them down and persuade them to focus on one issue, project or idea at a time. At first it can be a little unnerving for a shy person to try to restrain a Pinball client, but in the end it usually makes the relationship more congenial and productive. These three steps can boost your confidence when you communicate with a Pinball.

Step 1: Ask for the Pinball's specific goals and expectations

Pinballs are 'big picture' thinkers who often avoid focusing on the 'little pictures', or details, that are required to complete a task. To counter this tendency, cast your shyness aside and politely interrupt the Pinball's enthusiastic narrative. Ask him or her to immediately clarify problems, actions, goals and possible solutions.

Step 2: Ask the Pinball for a written plan

Pinballs love to 'brainstorm', but their unbridled creativity can lead a shy person who is hesitant to restrain them down a blind alley. To avoid this pitfall, first compliment their ingenuity to show them that you value 'idea people'. Then ask the Pinball to focus on a few, but not all, of the intermediate steps and details needed to complete the task.

A Pinball client may resist your request to write out his or her ideas with a comment such as 'I don't have time, and besides, that's what I pay you to do.' You can respond to this by saying, 'I wouldn't want to miss any of your great ideas, so if I can have about ten minutes of your time, perhaps we can plan out your idea together.'

Step 3: Ask the Pinball for additional clarification

Once a Pinball slows down long enough to think through an idea and define key steps, ask for further clarification. As a shy person, you may not always say what is on your mind, but this is another situation where speaking up is vital. Be sure to say you appreciate the Pinball's creativity, but that you want additional specific input.

Be ready to keep the Pinball focused on the immediate task when he or she comes up with yet another 'absolutely fabulous' idea. They have a million of them!

'Stallers' are passive clients

Passive clients are low-energy people who work slowly and produce little. They avoid risk-taking, decisions and commitments. Passive clients usually speak in a quiet voice and have closed body language. They offer almost no input or feedback, and rarely ask questions. Passive clients express little enthusiasm for new ideas and often say, 'This is the way we have always done it, so why change now?' These clients often take advantage of a shy person's inclination to avoid conflict. In other words, passive clients know that if they just keep dragging their feet, shy people will probably leave them alone.

Stallers fear risks, criticism and commitments

These passive clients work at a snail's pace and avoid taking even the smallest risk. They never seem to have enough information to make a decision or to get a commitment for a project so that you can go on to the next step. Stallers defer to the opinion of others and avoid taking personal responsibility by letting others make decisions.

Stallers leave you feeling frustrated by their slow rate of progress and lack of commitment. When Stallers fail to stick to a decision, or keep changing their minds, they decrease momentum and turn enthusiasm into discouragement. Stallers can make your life miserable because they know that most shy people will not confront them.

Help Stallers take small risks to overcome their fears

Stallers fear commitment and making mistakes. The bigger the decision or commitment, the longer they stall, hoping to avoid the situation entirely. These four steps will help build your confidence when dealing with Stallers.

Step 1: Break a big decision down into smaller, less risky decisions

Ask closed-ended 'yes or no'-type questions that allow the Staller to make a series of small decisions.

Step 2: Praise the Staller's decisions

Stallers need frequent praise and reinforcement about the decisions they make. Without going overboard, tell the Staller that you appreciate and support his or her decisions.

Step 3: Encourage the Staller to make the next decision

Stallers often need an extra push for them to continue with the decision-making process, but don't apply too much pressure or they will start stalling again.

Step 4: Apply gentle pressure

Sometimes Stallers give you no choice but to apply pressure for a decision to be made, and this might make you feel a little uncomfortable if you are shy. When this happens, be sure to ask for what you want and highlight the negative consequences of postponing the decision.

Stallers speed up when you show them that their decisions get results, but don't expect them to move too quickly even under the best of circumstances.

'Perfectionists' and 'Manipulators' are passive-aggressive clients

Passive-aggressive clients may be up one day and down the next day. When they get angry or frustrated, their unpredictable behaviour can turn nasty. Shy people are particularly vulnerable to passive-aggressive clients, because their troublesome behaviour is often subtle and difficult to anticipate. These clients are extremely hard to please.

Perfectionists set unattainable standards so nothing gets done

For the highly critical Perfectionists, few efforts will ever reach their nearly unattainable standards. They reject most work as a matter of course and question or admonish nearly every detail.

While Perfectionists are hard workers, they fear making mistakes so much that they miss deadlines, and often drive others mercilessly. They set unrealistic goals, and their compulsive desire for order, detail and logic kills enthusiasm and causes tremendous stress for those who work with them. These three steps will build your confidence when dealing with Perfectionists.

Step 1: Gain the Perfectionist's confidence with thorough preparation

Understanding the Perfectionist's need for order, oversensitivity to criticism and fear of mistakes can help you avoid confrontations with this passive-aggressive client. Make sure everything is in order and check every detail several times before you present work to the Perfectionist.

Step 2: Substantiate your work with facts and specific examples

Perfectionists love to test the competency of the people who work for them, so be ready to back up your work with solid facts and figures.

Step 3: Ask the Perfectionist for feedback

The Perfectionist will probably still find something wrong with your offering. However, rest assured that he or she will appreciate your attention to detail and desire to improve.

If you are lucky, the Perfectionist may even say that you did a good job, but don't bank on it!

Manipulators attempt to control and exploit others

These passive-aggressive clients mislead and stretch the facts. They often use confidential information or their job position to control the people they work with. These indirect communicators use veiled threats or implied promises to get what they want. They are secretive, unreliable, and can be vindictive when angry. Unfortunately for shy people, Manipulators know that they can usually play their destructive mind games with anyone except the most assertive communicators.

Manipulators foster distrust, encourage hostility, and lower general morale among colleagues. Clients with a passive-aggressive communication style blame you when things go wrong and take the credit when your efforts succeed. Dealing with the Manipulator may be difficult, but your job could be at stake. These three steps will increase your confidence when dealing with Manipulators.

Step 1: Never assume agreement with a Manipulator

Manipulators take advantage of the grey areas in communication whenever possible. In other words, a Manipulator will always interpret a statement to his or her advantage. Be on the alert for the Manipulator's vague comments, agreements or innuendos. Listen for phrases such as 'I suppose I might be able to . . .' or 'I guess I probably could . . .' When Manipulators fail to meet your expectations, they will often say, 'Well, I never said that I would actually do it.'

Step 2: Get it in writing when communicating with a Manipulator

Write a short memo recapping your discussions with a Manipulator. Get written and signed agreements for all promised work, including dates for payments. You can avoid many problems with Manipulators if you force them to pay strict attention to the 'small print'.

Step 3: Reject offers of confidential information or special treatment

Don't let a Manipulator tempt you with confidential information. The earlier you establish guidelines in the relationship, the less likely it is that the Manipulator will try to test your ethics.

If possible, avoid altogether clients who are Manipulators. Over time, the price of doing business with them is high and the returns are low.

Shy people can deal with difficult clients

Even if you are shy, you can succeed with difficult clients when you take control of the conversation and don't let them get away with their old tricks. Setting communication ground rules and using specific strategies will give you the confidence you need to work with these hard-to-handle clients. No one said it would be easy, but when you stand up to aggressive, passive and passive-aggressive clients, they will respect you and be easier to work with.

DOS AND DON'TS FOR DEALING WITH DIFFICULT CLIENTS

Do:

✓ Listen for a 'hidden agenda' when talking to difficult clients.

✓ Stay in close contact with your difficult clients.

✓ Tell your difficult clients what you want them to do and why.

✓ Gently but firmly confront your difficult clients.

✓ Focus on your difficult client's behaviour, not on his or her personality.

Don't:

✗ Overreact when difficult clients behave badly.

✗ Argue with your difficult clients.

✗ Discuss more than one problem at a time with a difficult client.

✗ Let difficult clients monopolize your time.

✗ Expect rapid improvements in behaviour from difficult clients.

16

Facilitating a training session

A facilitator is someone who makes learning easier

If your boss or client asked you to teach a sales, computer or other kind of workshop in your particular area of expertise, would you know what to do? Even if you are shy or have never, ever taught in your life, you can excel in this extremely rewarding form of public speaking. To successfully facilitate a workshop, you must break down complicated skills or concepts into easily mastered units and then motivate participants to learn.

Defining learning objectives

Like other forms of public speaking, facilitating a successful training session requires organization as well as a willingness to share specialist knowledge. Thus, shy people like you often make excellent facilitators because you are apt to carefully prepare your workshops rather than rely on your impromptu speaking skills.

To organize your training session, first define your learning objectives by asking yourself the following questions:

- Who are the people attending the workshop?
- What level of skills do the participants have?
- What new skills will participants have after they finish the training?
- What are the three to five most important skills the participants need to learn?
- What prior skills do participants need to know before learning new skills?
- How long will the training session last?
- How many participants will be at the session?
- What hand-outs, audiovisual aids and props will help participants learn?
- What special circumstances or issues do you need to address in the session?

- Where will you train the group?
- Why is it important that the participants learn these skills?
- In what ways will the participants benefit personally and professionally?
- How will this training session increase productivity or profits of the participants' business or company?

Writing helps you define the group's learning objectives

Writing down the main ideas that you want your group to learn will help you clarify the information you need to present. A specifically defined objective facilitates learning.

How many learning objectives should you have per session?

Generally, the fewer learning objectives you include, the more time you have for example, practice and feedback. Three or four learning objectives are sufficient for a two-hour session. Five to ten learning objectives are ample for a half-day or full-day training session.

Use the trainer's motto

The following formula highlights the three basic parts of a training session:

1 Tell them what you are going to tell them.
2 Tell them.
3 Tell them what you've told them.

Just as you learned in Chapter 12, the introduction to your workshop needs an attention-grabbing opening. Then you can add a brief overview of learning objectives, topics and benefits. The body of the training session requires the most time and consists of a lecture, demonstration, exercises and practice. The conclusion includes questions and answers, a short recap of the main points, and a closing statement that motivates the participants to use their new skills in the workplace.

Part 1: Tell them what you are going to tell them (5–10 minutes)

    Step 1: Use an engaging opening.
    Step 2: Highlight the learning objectives.
    Step 3: Identify the benefits for the participants.
    Step 4: Offer a thumbnail biography of yourself.

Step 5: Clarify what you expect from the group.
Step 6: Explain about breaks and the location of the toilets.

Step 1: Use an engaging opening

Even if you consider yourself a little shy, you will exude confidence in front of the group you are training when your introduction is strong and smooth. Knowing what you are going to say in your introduction and practising it several times aloud can really help to control your nervousness. You don't have to memorize your opening statement word for word; simply communicate the main ideas to your audience. Write your ideas on cards if necessary.

Begin your introduction with a dramatic fact or statement or an evocative question that grabs your audience's attention and focuses it on the subject of the training session. The sooner you identify the group's learning needs and explain how the participants are going to benefit from the session, the more you will facilitate their learning.

Step 2: Highlight the learning objectives

Once you have the participants' attention, tell them their learning objectives. By defining objectives, you set the training session's agenda.

Step 3: Identify the benefits for the participants

Teaching people who are not motivated to learn is an uphill battle, so be sure to identify the benefits, or 'W-I-I-F-M' ('What's in it for me?'), of the workshop. Explain how the information in this session will help the participants in the future.

Step 4: Offer a thumbnail biography of yourself

Standing before a group of workshop participants can be nerve-racking. However, this is no time to be shy, because you need to quickly establish your credibility. Unless someone introduces you or everyone knows you, take less than a minute to tell the group who you are and why you are leading this training session.

Keep your biography short and directly connected to the training session. Include a few words about how the skills you are going to present in the workshop have helped you.

Step 5: Clarify what you expect from the group

Do not let any of your old shy habits prevent you from letting the participants know who is calling the shots in your workshop. Most people will happily comply with any rules or expectations that you mention in your introduction.

You learned in Chapter 3 that laughter can make people more receptive, so smile and end your introduction with something like:

> *'Finally, if you want to get good marks in today's workshop, you must laugh at my jokes! Any questions? Great! Let's get started.'*

Step 6: Explain about breaks and the location of the toilets

For workshops that last longer than an hour, take a moment to tell the participants when you will take breaks and where the toilets are. It may sound odd, but people are particularly sensitive to these issues. An old trainer's motto goes something like this: 'The adult mind can only absorb to the extent that the bladder can endure.'

Part 2: Tell them

Step 1: Present an 'icebreaker' exercise that relates to a skill or concept.
Step 2: Introduce a new skill or concept.
Step 3: Demonstrate the new skill or concept.
Step 4: Get the participants to practise the new skill or concept.
Step 5: Elicit feedback, offer help, and answer questions.

Step 1: Present an 'icebreaker' exercise that relates to a skill or concept

This may come as a shock, but you – the facilitator – are probably not the only nervous person in a workshop. An 'icebreaker' is a short exercise that gives the participants an opportunity to mentally 'warm up' before they learn something new. Plus, if you are a little nervous, an icebreaker exercise is a good way to start the workshop in an interactive way. It is important that an icebreaker exercise ties into the learning objectives of the workshop and reinforces the knowledge necessary to learn a new skill.

Step 2: Introduce a new skill or concept

Present the new skill or concept with a short and simple explanation. Use words that everyone understands and be sure not to assume too much knowledge on the part of the participants. Watch carefully for confused looks or participants looking around at one another.

111

Step 3: Demonstrate the new skill or concept

Now is the time to demonstrate the new skill or concept. At this point, you might feel a little uneasy standing in front of a group. One way to build your confidence is to practise the demonstration several times before the workshop.

Be sure to explain how the new skill fits into the learning objectives of the workshop. It is also the time for participants to ask any questions about the skill and its application.

Step 4: Get the participants to practise the new skill or concept

Ask the participants to practise the new skill in pairs or small groups. (The other shy people in the workshop may need a little extra time and assistance to find a group.)

Circulate around the room to check that the participants are practising the new skill correctly. You may see other shy people feeling a little uncomfortable during this part of your workshop. If necessary, gently guide them through the steps of the exercise until they can do it on their own. When you are helping others, you'll forget your own nervousness.

PARTICIPANTS LEARN BY DOING

Experienced facilitators know that people learn by doing and that they want practical information with immediate applications. Participants generally want challenging activities, enjoy sharing relevant experiences, and are most successful when they build on something they already know. Studies show that most learning takes place when participants practise and apply their new skills. Use the following activities and exercises to involve the participants and make your workshop 'hands on'.

- Group discussion.
- Paired and small-group activities.
- Flip chart presentation.
- Hand-outs and worksheets.

- Panels.
- Role playing.

- Questionnaires.
- Games.

Step 5: Elicit feedback, offer help, and answer questions

Processing exercises is a vital part of the learning process. It allows participants to offer feedback about what the exercise taught them.

You can also evaluate the effectiveness of the exercise and see who 'got it' and who didn't. You can offer additional assistance or suggestions to those who need a little extra help and address any remaining questions about the skill or exercise. Once you have completed this step, have a short break. Then introduce the next new skill or concept.

Handling troublesome participants

If you are a shy or inexperienced facilitator, your workshop can end up on the rocks if you underestimate or ignore certain troublesome participants. The 'Machine Gunner', 'Expert', 'Chatterbox' or 'Groaner' are examples of uncooperative people who can quickly disrupt your training session, undermine your credibility, and ruin the learning experience for the other attendees. As a facilitator, it is your obligation to assertively handle these difficult people. You may wish you could just ignore problem participants, but they will not go away unless you take an assertive stance.

Answering the Machine Gunner

Aggressive participants like the Machine Gunner love to challenge nearly everything you say with a series of rapid questions. They demand proof with hard data, but rarely let you finish one answer before hitting you with another volley of questions. Their strategy is to engage you in verbal combat, make you lose your cool, and seem an idiot. As you learned in Chapter 7, the secret it to remain calm and to politely interrupt them.

Outsmarting the Expert

Experts want to steal the spotlight from you and take control of your training session. They love to tell long-winded stories and talk about their achievements to build themselves up at your expense. They want recognition, so give them a little of what they want, and promise to give them some attention later.

Quieting the Chatterbox

A Chatterbox disrupts a session by attempting to draw attention away from you and refocus it on himself or herself. Since Chatterboxes talk instead of listen, they often miss instructions and distract others. If you are shy, you might be inclined to let them continue their negative behaviour, but if you do, they can end up ruining exercises and discussion activities. In addition, they can slow down the progress of others.

Neutralizing the Groaner

Groaners stall and complain throughout every activity or exercise with the hope that they can avoid doing any work. Their goal is to undermine your credibility by implying that the training session or exercise is not worth their time or trouble. If the Groaner's negative behaviour persists even after you have gently asked for his or her co-operation, then give the group a short self-directed activity, walk up to the Groaner, and quietly ask him or her to step outside the room with you.

Part 3: Tell them what you have told them (15–30 minutes)

Step 1: Prepare a question-and-answer session.
Step 2: Summarize the main skills and concepts.
Step 3: Close with a bang.

Although you prepared and presented a well-organized training session, you still need to provide an opportunity for the participants to ask any remaining questions. In addition, summarizing the main points for the participants helps them to remember the skills they have just learned. Finally, you need to give an uplifting close to the session that motivates the participants to continue learning after they leave your training workshop.

Step 1: Prepare a question-and-answer session

Shy or new trainers sometimes feel nervous about taking questions, and so end their sessions with a cursory 'Any questions?' Properly used, the question-and-answer session can provide an excellent opportunity for you to clarify and reinforce your main points.

Use the following techniques to answer questions more effectively:

✓ Restate the question so that everyone can hear it.
✓ Paraphrase a long question into ten words or less.
✓ Keep your answers short and to the point.
✓ Anticipate and prepare responses ahead of time for 'devil's advocate' questions.
✓ If you do not know the answer, open it up to the group or to the person asking the question. You can always say that you will try to find out the answer and contact him or her later.
✓ If the question is off the subject or of a personal nature, you can say, 'That question falls outside the scope of our session today. I'd be happy to talk to you after our session concludes.'
✓ Be ready with some questions of your own to stimulate participation.

Step 2: Summarize the main skills and concepts

Repetition is a vital part of learning, especially for participants sitting in an all-day training session. Restate the main skills and concepts of your session without going into detail. If you have the time, you can rephrase them as questions and give the group an oral quiz.

Step 3: Close with a bang

You have about a minute remaining in your training session. The only thing you have left to do is to acknowledge the participants' fine efforts and to send them out of the room eager to use what you have taught them. Your closing statement should summarize everything you have said during the session. Professional trainers often write and memorize their closing statement so that it gets the desired response: big smiles, laughs and a warm round of applause. The 'closing' can consist of an inspirational quotation, some short anecdotes, or a 'signature' poem.

Don't forget to thank your audience with something like this:

'Thank you, everyone. You've been a great group and I hope you enjoyed today's workshop!'

115

Facilitating a training session builds communication confidence

When you present clearly defined concepts and skills in an interactive workshop, you will motivate the participants and facilitate their learning. All your planning and careful attention to detail will pay off in a smooth and organized presentation that says you are a seasoned and confident trainer. However, it is after you end the workshop and get a big round of applause that you receive your greatest reward – the gratification you feel when a participant tells you:

'This is the best workshop I've ever been to.'

TEN WAYS TO FACILITATE ADULT LEARNING

1 Identify specific training needs before planning your workshop.
2 Present practical skills that fulfil previously identified needs.
3 Create active discussion as well as problem-solving and role-playing exercises.
4 Allow short opportunities for comments and questions throughout the workshop.
5 Use props and visual aids to illustrate ideas and concepts.
6 Take frequent short breaks.
7 Make a workshop agenda and stick to it.
8 Encourage participants to share their experiences and expertise as it pertains to the workshop objectives.
9 When working in groups, change group leaders frequently.
10 Put extra ideas and information on hand-outs or in an appendix.

17

'Sharing meals' and 'Talking big deals'

'Let's do lunch'

While the popular invitation to share a meal is probably one of the most commonly uttered phrases in business today, it can leave a shy person with acute indigestion. 'Power breakfasts', two-hour lunches, after-work drinks, or full-course dinners at upmarket restaurants are popular venues for discussing deals. However, many shy people avoid these important business opportunities because they do not know what to say before, during and after the meal. You might be surprised to find that discussing a business proposition while sharing a meal is an enjoyable and productive way to do business.

FIVE RULES OF CONVERSATION AND BUSINESS DINING

Rule 1: Know your business aim.
Rule 2: Balance how much time you talk and listen.
Rule 3: Know when – and when not – to talk business.
Rule 4: Move smoothly from small talk to your business topic.
Rule 5: Consume and converse at a comfortable rate.

Rule 1: Know your business aim

Whether you are meeting for a 'power breakfast', lunch, after-work drinks or a gourmet dinner, remember the purpose of your meeting. Perhaps your client wants to discuss a new marketing plan. Maybe he or she needs background information for a sales presentation later in the day. Often the main purpose of eating together is simply to get to know each other better and to build rapport. Remember that many of the conversational tips you learned in Parts 1 and 2 of this book also apply to business dining. Whatever your reasons for eating together, be sure you always keep your business aim on the front burner.

117

Rule 2: Balance how much time you talk and listen

Sharing a meal allows the dining companions an opportunity to get to know each other better. If you are shy, you may find it easier to ask questions and let your companion do most of the talking. However, talking about yourself is equally important if the other person is going to get to know you. If you remain too quiet, you may appear shy and make the other person feel uncomfortable. The fastest way to build rapport while dining with someone is for you and your companion to talk and listen at about the same rate. I use this rule of thumb: I want the other person to know as much about me as I know about him or her.

Rule 3: Know when – and when not – to talk business

Opinions differ about the 'right time' to discuss business issues when dining. Some people like to get right down to business and others like to warm up with a little small talk. A safe rule to follow is this: the shorter the meal time, the sooner you can discuss business. The more time you have to eat, the longer the period of small talk before getting down to business. For example, at breakfast meetings, feel free to discuss business topics with a minimum of small talk beforehand. At a lunch meeting, small talk usually takes place up to the time of ordering the meal. Finally, at a one-to-one or small-group dinner meeting, most people prefer to relax for half-an-hour or so before discussing business.

Following the lead of your host or client is wise, unless he or she is reluctant to discuss business until your meal is almost over. If you are the 'all-business' type, and your client likes to chat a bit before talking business, then be ready to make some small talk about your forthcoming holiday or hobby. However, you can keep small talk to a minimum by sharing some information and then asking your dining companion a 'bridging question' to move the conversation closer to your business topic.

Rule 4: Move smoothly from small talk to your business topic

Tact is vital when you want to change from small talk to a business topic. A shy person may make the error of abruptly jumping to the business topic – this is a mistake because sudden conversational transitions can put off a dining companion. 'Bridging' allows you to gracefully steer the conversation over two or even three subjects to get to your business topic. To bridge smoothly, listen for key words or phrases from your dining companion that somehow relate to your business topic. The connections between topics may be a stretch, but if possible, hook them together so that you can change topics without sounding pushy or aggressive.

Rule 5: Consume and converse at a comfortable rate

Few things are more irritating than sharing a meal with someone who eats too quickly or too slowly. Ideally, both diners should begin and end their meal at about the same time. As the meal progresses, gauge the other person's progress, and speed up or slow down so you reach dessert or coffee together.

You can help a fast eater relax by asking open-ended questions that encourage him or her to talk about a business topic or other subject. As the other person talks, take the opportunity to eat more of your meal. Listen carefully for opportunities to build rapport and identify his or her specific business needs.

For a dining companion who spends more time talking than nibbling, you need to become more actively involved in the conversation. Tell a short story or interesting example to illustrate a point the other person has made. Then follow it up with a point or two of your own, and connect it to a business topic that you want to discuss. This shows that you are a good listener, have something to add to the conversation, and are ready to talk business. Meanwhile, you give your dining companion a chance to finish his or her meal. By the time the waiter or waitress removes the dessert plates from the table and serves coffee, your business conversation should be coming to a close.

'Picking other people's brains'

Asking for advice and information is a perfectly legitimate reason to invite someone to share a meal, as long as you make that purpose clear in your invitation. For some shy people, 'picking someone's brain' may sound a bit forward, but let me share this experience with you. Two entrepreneurs, one of whom describes himself as shy, invited me to dinner with the express purpose of learning all they

119

could from me about writing, publishing and public speaking. For nearly two hours they asked me dozens of questions and I answered them as best I could – between bites! Ideally, the information I shared helped my dining companions move closer to their goals as speakers and authors, and in the meantime I benefited from the meeting in two ways: I met two smart people with whom I am now doing business, and I had a delicious meal. That's a good deal for everyone!

After you have finished talking business, don't just bolt from the table waving the signed agreement in your hand. Etiquette requires some additional light conversation before you end the meal.

Dining for business builds relationships

Most people choose to do business with people they like, and what better way to spend time together than over an enjoyable meal? For a shy person like you, it may take some extra confidence-building self-talk to suggest sharing a meal with a business acquaintance, but it will be worth it. You may achieve a monetary reward right away, but you'll be building a business relationship that – with a little luck and persistence – may lead to a major contract at some point in the future!

The Sixteen Biggest Mistakes Shy People Make While Dining with Clients

1 Waiting too long to bring up a business topic.
2 Only talking business (unless that's the client's style).
3 Revealing confidential information.
4 Arguing about controversial topics.
5 Getting nervous and talking too much or too little.
6 Overindulging in alcohol and/or food.
7 Forgetting good table manners.
8 Trying to impress clients with too many details.
9 Gossiping about competitors.
10 Using inappropriate language or humour.
11 Failing to show interest in the other person.
12 Failing to talk about a wide variety of topics.
13 Failing to listen for or suggest topics for future business discussions.
14 Failing to make smooth transitions from small talk to business topics.
15 Failing to build trust, and likeability through a balance of self-disclosure and listening.
16 Hard-selling their product or service.

18

'Networking' at conferences and meetings

The aim of networking is to expand your business contacts

In the mid-1980s an ex-hippie-turned-entrepreneur in the United States hosted what he described as 'networking' parties. The purpose of these business get-togethers was for people in different professions and with different interests to exchange information, services and contacts. Like hungry sharks, hundreds of job-seekers, salespeople, entrepreneurs and other motivated people consumed by the score one another's business cards, telephone numbers and names. Their hope was that one or two networking contacts might lead to a job, a referral or even a big contract. After a couple of hours of this conversational 'feeding frenzy', everyone left and the party was over. The following week, the process began again. Networking became a primary strategy for people who wanted to exchange information or services with individuals, groups or institutions.

Slowly, this movement has started to take off in the United Kingdom also.

How can networking help you?

No matter what profession you are in, networking can help you achieve many of your career and business goals. You may feel shy about meeting strangers and convincing them that they want to help you find a job, make a sale or meet a new client. However, learning how to effectively network can only help your business and career. Networking gives you the opportunity to:

✓ Be a professional resource for others.
✓ Build up your business contacts.
✓ Exchange business cards.
✓ Expand employment opportunities.
✓ Find new clients or business.
✓ Give and receive referrals.
✓ Hear emerging industry trends.

✓ Learn about professional associations.
✓ Make friends with other professionals.
✓ Meet industry 'movers and shakers'.
✓ Mentor others new in your profession.
✓ Share your expertise and insights.

Where are the best places to network?

Today, networking is more popular than ever and you can network anywhere and at any time. Professional associations provide numerous opportunities for members to network during meetings. The following list includes just a few of the many places where you can meet people and try out your networking skills:

- On planes and at airports.
- Association meetings and conventions.
- Business and career workshops.
- Local voluntary organizations.
- Fund-raising events.
- Health clubs.
- Industry-awards dinners.
- Parties.
- Reunions.
- Social/business get-togethers.
- Trade shows.

Network in informal situations

Not all successful networkers focus their efforts in large groups. For example, I know one shy solicitor who works with small-business owners. He networks at his local wine bar, in the lift in the block of flats he lives in, at dinner parties, while working out at the gym, or anywhere else that he meets people in informal situations. He doesn't 'hard-sell' or pressurize anyone, but instead simply lets people know that if they have a legal question about their small businesses, they can talk to him – at no charge. If they find his advice helpful, they may retain him for a case or refer him to someone else with a small business who needs a solicitor.

Four steps to networking

Even if you are shy, you can still meet people, start conversations and make business contacts by using the conversational skills you learned in Chapters 4 and 5. Starting to network is easy if you think of the task as having four parts. First, introduce yourself and briefly tell others what you do. Second, find out about the other person's business. Third, mingle with a message, and fourth, follow up. Let's take one step at a time.

Step 1: Master the ten-second introduction

Assume that people attending formal networking functions or any get-together want to meet you. The problem is, how do you introduce yourself, tell others what you do, and find out about them? The solution is to master the ten-second introduction. This is what you can do:

- Take the initiative. Establish eye contact, smile, and offer to shake hands. Then, in a friendly voice, slowly say your first and last name. If your name is unusual or familiar in some way, suggest a way to remember it. I often say, 'Hi, my name is Don Gabor – like Zsa Zsa Gabor.'

- In a few words, tell others 'what you do' and 'who you do it for'. Avoid professional titles or technical descriptions. For example, I usually say, 'I write books and run workshops for people who want to improve their interpersonal communication skills.' Since I want to make myself memorable and let others know my unique approach to the subject, I often add, 'I teach people how to make small talk. In fact, I'm the "small-talk expert"!'

- If the person asks a follow-up question based on what you have told them, briefly explain the benefits of your product or service. For example, I say, 'I help salespeople increase their referral and sales through networking.' Or 'I teach ways to deal with difficult colleagues and clients.' Or 'I help shy people become more confident in social and business situations.'

Networking tip: Keep your introductions conversational. Avoid a 'canned' or memorized benefits statement. Just say how you help others to achieve their goals.

Step 2: Ask about the other person's business

Some people you meet at networking functions may be shy too, so be ready to ask them a few questions to get the conversation going. If the other person has not introduced himself or herself, say, 'And you are ... ?' Or 'What is your name?'

Networking tip: Put your name badge on the right side of your jacket or top so people can easily read it as they shake hands with you.

Step 3: Mingle with a message, not a sales pitch

What do you say after you introduce yourself to a stranger? Most shy people fear that they cannot keep a networking session going. To solve this dilemma, prepare a list of at least five issues, trends and topics that relate to your business before you attend the networking session. Then formulate a 'message' and relate your skills or profession to these topics of conversation. For example, perhaps you own a restaurant and are networking at a catering fair. Here are some related topics and trends that you might list:

✓ Articles in trade magazines.
✓ Banquets, parties and weddings.
✓ Ethnic cuisine within hotels.
✓ Health and diet issues in catering.
✓ Hiring a chef and staff training.
✓ Hotel catering association programmes.
✓ On-line marketing.
✓ Speciality foods for catered events.

Networking is not hard-selling

You learned in Chapter 13 that most people do not like a 'hard-sell'. The same is true when networking. Of course you'd like to find a new client or make a sale, but your primary goal is simply to make business contacts. When you share information about industry issues with others attending the function, you'll keep the conversation going naturally and will make valuable contacts at the same time. You will also reveal more about what you do and find out more about the other person. Be sure to:

✓ Elicit information about the other person's business by asking both closed and open-ended questions.
✓ Subtly blow your own trumpet by stressing how people benefit from your skills or service.
✓ Link your skills and services to the other person's business needs.

Use questions like these to keep the conversation moving at a networking function:

'How did you get involved in the ... business?'

'Who are the people here who influence your business the most?'

Networking tip: Showing interest in the people you meet while networking creates rapport and makes those people feel comfortable talking to you. Remember, most people prefer to do business with those they know, like and trust.

Step 4: Follow up and make networking pay off

For most shy people, suggesting a follow-up telephone call or meeting after the initial contact requires some extra effort. However, following up with contacts is one of the most important yet least exercised skills in networking. Building a lasting business relationship begins with an invitation to talk at another time.

Networking tip: If you still feel shy about networking, then view it this way. Other people have as much or more to gain from meeting you as you have from meeting them. When you help others achieve their goals, you are networking in the truest sense of the word and, in the end, you will reap the rewards.

Networking pays off in more ways than one

Although you may be shy, now you know how to network for more business contacts in social and business situations. Even if the people you meet don't become clients right away, don't be discouraged. As you continue to expand your contacts and refer potential clients to the other people you meet, your networking will pay off in many ways. Not only will it help you and your associates to achieve your professional goals, but it will boost your communication skills and confidence too.

TEN NETWORKING STRATEGIES THAT INCREASE CONTACTS AND CONFIDENCE

Networking strategies build business relationships and increase your income.

1 **Develop a networking attitude.** Actively network whenever you are in business and social situations. Don't just talk to your friends and colleagues.

2 **Move around the room.** Don't be a 'potted plant' that remains rooted to the sofa. Meet as many people as possible.

3 **Take the initiative.** Be the first to introduce yourself to others, especially to successful people who have large networks.

4 **'The sweetest sound in any language is a person's name'.** Repeat the person's name as you meet, as well as during, and especially at the end of, the conversation.

5 **Make yourself memorable.** Master the art of the ten-second introduction. Tell people who you are and the products or services you provide.

6 **Discover people's needs.** Ask open-ended questions to uncover specific needs. If you can't fill the other person's needs, try to find the name of someone who can.

7 **Be friendly, conversational and show interest.** People do business with, and refer business to, those they like and trust. The sooner you build rapport and offer to help others, the faster your networking will pay off in more referrals and sales.

8 **Be a host and facilitator.** Make others feel more comfortable and facilitate networking by introducing associates and guests. Networking is about helping others make connections.

9 **Have fun, but don't forget your manners.** Networking at parties is enjoyable and rewarding if you remember to use your common sense. One drink too many, a joke in poor taste, or a sexist remark can destroy any chances for future business.

10 **Follow up.** Keep in contact with the people you meet. Send articles and other information related to a person's interests or needs.

Conclusion

Talking with confidence means you're no longer shy

Your communication skills are like your muscles: the more you exercise them, the more powerful they become. As you increase your ability to talk in social and business situations, your confidence will also grow stronger, and you'll feel less shy. At times you may still feel nervous on the inside, but on the outside you communicate an interested, interesting, confident and friendly image to everyone you meet – friends, family, clients and strangers. Each time you practise the techniques in this book, you will move one step closer to overcoming your lifelong struggle with shyness. Talking with confidence will lead you to many new social and business opportunities, but the most important reward is when you say to yourself, 'I used to be shy – but not any more!'

Index

argument: avoiding 45;
changing topics 42–3;
defusing at parties 36–7;
polite disagreement 42;
reacting to quarrelsome
boors 40–2; silence 44

body language: confidence 62;
distance 20; eye contact and
smiles 19, 20; things to
avoid 20, 32
business meals: asking advice
119–20; five rules 117–19;
sixteen mistakes 121

compliments 5
conversation *see also* small
talk: asking others about
themselves 54–5; evading
toxic topics 43–4; expressing
views 10, 32; feeding 52;
mixing at parties 28–31;
negative and positive notes
54–6; reacting to
quarrelsome boors 40–2

difficult people: dos and don'ts
107; Intimidators 99–102;
Manipulators 106–7;
meetings 71–3; parties 36–8;
Perfectionists 105–6; Pinballs
102–3; Stallers 103–5;

workshops 113–14

facilitating: the core of the
workshop 111–14; defining
learning objectives 108–9;
difficult people 113–14;
learning by doing 112–13;
opening overview 109–11;
summing up 114–15; ten tips
116

Gardner, Ava 13
groups: mixing at parties
28–32

Heggen, Thomas: *Mister
Roberts* 75
hobbies and interests 7
humour: appreciating others'
11–12; offensive 13; self-
effacing 12–13; telling
stories 12, 14

independence 6
introductions: basic rules 35;
groups 31; networking
123–4; remembering 21;
using others' names 31, 32
invitations 23–4

job interviews: confidence
61–2; employers' needs
63–4; interviewing the

129